THE
SUGAR
DETOX
PLAN

First published in Great Britain in 2016 by Modern Books
An imprint of Elwin Street Limited
3 Percy Street
London WIT IDE
www.elwinstreet.com

ISBN 978-1-906761-68-4
6 7 8 9 10   5 4 3 2 1

Translator: Alison Tunley
Culinary consultant: Drew Smith

Originally published under the title:
Zucker – Der Heimliche Killer
By Dr Kurt Mosetter, Dr Wolfgang Simon,
Thorsten Probost and Anna Cavelius
© 2014 by Gräfe und Unzer Verlag

Printed in China

THE SUGAR DETOX PLAN

The essential 3-step plan for breaking your sugar habit

Dr Kurt Mosetter, Dr Wolfgang Simon,
Thorsten Probost and Anna Cavelius

'Like pop stars, food groups gain and lose popularity. Eggs were demonized – salmonella and cholesterol poisoning seemed inevitable – but now, thanks to comprehensive modern evidence they have been rehabilitated, and are now considered a 'super food'.

The low carbohydrate diet was invented in 1797 by Dr John Rollo, the army physician who treated diabetic patients with a low-starch diet, as opposed to the high-sugar diet popular at the time. William Banting popularized the diet in 1863, but the regime fell out of favour in 1953, due to some flawed science which was quoted endlessly in journals and guidelines.

It is substantially due to luminaries such as John Yudkin, Gary Taubes and Robert Lustig that the climate is changing. Now the medical community and the general public are waking up to the fact that sugar is poisonous, and is to blame for many common (and expensive) illnesses suffered by society. *The Sugar Detox Plan* provides practical advice, backed by scientific principles, on how to survive in a world where sugar is ubiquitous.'
Professor David Haslam, Chair, National Obesity Forum

'Sugar causes diseases: unrelated to their calories and unrelated to the attendant weight gain. It's an independent primary-risk factor.'
Professor Robert H. Lustig, University of California, San Francisco

'It's addictive, it's everywhere and scientists are coming round to thinking it does us no good at all.'
Helen Rumbelow, *The Times*

'Sugar is a greater enemy to the body than salt: added sugars in processed foods are more likely to cause high blood pressure, stroke and heart disease.'
Lizzie Parry, *Daily Mail*

'Sugar is basically a socially acceptable, legal, recreational drug, with deadly consequences – and like with any drug addiction, you have to have a flexible but structured plan to beat it.'
goop.com

'Move over salt and hypertension, you've got competition. Sugar, as it turns out, is just as much of a silent killer.'
Kristin Kirkpatrick, *Huffington Post*

CONTENTS

INTRODUCTION

Dr. Kurt Mosetter, Dr. Wolfgang Simon, Thorsten Probost and Anna Cavelius

Ask most people you know, and they'll say sweet things taste good and make life fun – but they probably aren't thinking of their teeth when saying it. Nor are they thinking about associated risk factors such as abdominal fat, or diabetes. About Alzheimer's or attention deficit hyperactivity disorder (ADHD). And it is very unlikely that they are thinking about a metabolic addiction whose power is comparable to that of nicotine or alcohol, and is equally difficult to escape.

In these times of excess food supply in the affluent countries of the world, the love of all things sweet has long since lost its innocence. Experts warn that sugar is one of the most dangerous poisons of our age. Furthermore, sugar consumption has risen dramatically over the last fifty years, trebling worldwide, and it continues to rise. According to the National Diet and Nutrition Survey, the average British adult (aged 19–64) consumes 59 g of sugar per day – a massive 21.5 kg per year. Over the course of human evolution sugar has been an important source of energy, but today it is a cheap, constantly available foodstuff with an unlimited shelf-life.

The human metabolism still works to a prehistoric rhythm, but our world and our diets have changed radically since that time, and therefore we find ourselves with a significant problem today. The overproduction of foodstuffs and the ability to store foods are both signs of the materially affluent Western lifestyle and, in their wake, they bring fatal diseases such as diabetes and can contribute to neurodegenerative disorders such as Alzheimer's. Recent studies show that sugar, in the quantities available to us now, not only makes us fat, tired and listless, but also has an extremely damaging effect on our bodies overall. In the long term it can alter your metabolism so that sweet things actually fuel your cravings for even more sugar.

Now for the good news: help is at hand! *The Sugar Detox Plan* brings you a simple, three-step programme to living a sugar-free life and breaking the sugar dependency for good.

Our withdrawal plan is, above all, a feel-good programme, carefully designed and arranged to make your sugar 'cold turkey' pass by easily and without stress. In following the plan your metabolism will heal almost incidentally and any pre-existing conditions relating to a metabolic disorder will likely also show a marked improvement.

The advice contained in *The Sugar Detox Plan* is the result of a long-standing and close collaboration between the authors, drawing on the extensive practical medical experience of Dr Kurt Mosetter, years of biochemical research by Dr Wolfgang Simon and the practical investigations of journalist Anna Cavelius.

The team's scientific findings are underlined and supported by the culinary creativity of Thorsten Probost, gourmet chef at the five-star Burg Vital health resort in Lech, Austria. His recipes will help you re-educate your dysfunctional sugar metabolism without having to give up on sweetness altogether.

We hope you enjoy following the plan as much as we enjoyed putting it together, and that you achieve the same excellent results that we have seen time and time again in people of all ages and fitness levels. Above all, we wish you every success and the very best of health!

Kurt Mosetter, Wolfgang Simon, Thorsten Probost and Anna Cavelius

1

Your Relationship with Sugar

It's time for you to re-evaluate your relationship with sugar. In order to do that, you need to know about the different types of sugar that exist, and where they feature in the foods that you eat. More importantly, you need to understand how these sugars affect your body when eaten in excessive quantities.

SWEET TEMPTATION

Next time you go shopping, take a look in your basket. If there is a list of ingredients on a packet, the chances are sugar is on it.

Having found its way into the obvious (chocolate bars) to the less obvious (muesli bars) – and thanks to its secretive inclusion in breads, pastas and the many processed meals of the fast-food industry – sugar makes up the bulk of the energy that we eat.

CONDITIONED BY SWEETNESS

Sugar gives us a quick hit of energy. It makes us feel fed and happy. This is genetic. We learn it from our mother's breast milk and baby milk formulas.

Our very first taste in the world is one of sweetness, and numerous studies have shown that babies do not usually like sour, salty or bitter flavours. We only develop our interest in other flavours as we get older and our bodies (and taste buds) mature. And just as we no longer need nourishment from our mother's milk when we grow up, we don't really need sugar either, but we are accustomed and psychologically habituated. In our minds, *sweet* equals *good*.

Tasting Sweetness

Sweetness is also an unusual and powerful flavour. The other primary tastes (saltiness, bitterness, sourness and the savoury flavours known as umami) involve the nose and the many sensory labels we call smell. Sweetness, however, occurs solely in the mouth and seems to communicate directly with the brain, immediately triggering a variety of physical responses.

We have as many as 2,000 to 5,000 taste buds covering our tongues, but while we have as many as 25 different receptors or buds for detecting bitterness, with sugar there is just one – although that sweet taste bud can differentiate between different kinds of sugars. Each of the basic flavours create different reactions and responses in the body, but sweetness delivers a powerful surge of endogenous opiates (also known as endorphins). The body's own natural gratification system springs instantly into action. We cannot help but create an association between sweetness and bliss, contentment, good humour and relaxation.

HIDDEN DANGERS

These days everyone is well aware that eating too many sugary foods can contribute to weight gain. However, what many of us don't know is that the levels of sugar consumption we see in an average diet can lead to much more than simply gaining a few pounds. With a high intake of sugar there is a vastly increased risk of developing type 2 diabetes, and errant blood sugar levels sparked by too much sugar in the diet have been implicated as contributing factors in heart disease, dementia and even in some cancers.

Doctors and the medical professionals no longer think of sugar as a harmless stimulant, but believe that the substance creates a dependency in much the same way as alcohol and nicotine. In fact, recent studies have shown that our cravings for sweet things such as chocolate or ice cream are similar to the desire for a hit from other narcotics. On satisfying a craving for sugar the same opioids are triggered in the brain, creating a calming, relaxing, anaesthetizing mood as can be found when a person takes morphine. And as we shall see, these chemicals can permanently alter the function of our brains and our reactions to all kinds of foods.

HOW SUGAR GETS YOU HOOKED

The relationship between sugar and the brain depends on complex networks that are crucial in controlling our mood, weight and metabolic system – and therefore our overall health. When the control mechanisms for our sugar metabolism are damaged and unregulated, a shortage of sugar can lead to constant eating and uncontrollable food cravings. Rectifying the problem is not straight forward, however, since some scientists now believe that indulgent sugary foods should be considered addictive substances, like alcohol or cocaine, because sugar triggers the same reactions in the brain as these intoxicants.

Addictive Reactions

In 2001, Bart Hoebel, professor of psychology at Princeton University, presented a study in which he demonstrated that the sugar in our diets makes us dependent. Hoebel was an expert in the neuroscientific foundations of addictive behaviour, and he was convinced that, in the long term, the brain responds with an addictive reaction to 'feel-good' foods such as sugar and fat.

Similarly, the renowned psychiatrist and leading researcher in the complexities of the human brain, Nora Volkow, director of the US National Institute on Drug Abuse, also discovered a significant overlap in the effects of drugs and nutrition on the brain. Using magnetic imaging techniques, Volkow illustrated how the brains of overweight people, drug addicts and alcoholics share a number of striking similarities. This is backed up by research from the Central Institute for Mental Health in Mannheim, Germany, which demonstrates that significantly overweight people tend to react far more strongly to pictures of foods containing sugar, than to pictures of healthy food. Compared with normal-weight test subjects, obese participants showed far greater activity in the nucleus accumbens, the area known as the brain's 'pleasure centre'.

If sugar is addictive, it explains why we are so fond of the sugar-flour combinations found in bread or pastries, and our predilection for ready meals and fizzy drinks. We don't actually eat these items because we like them, but because we have the *feeling* that we like them.

THE ROAD TO DEPENDENCY

The initial steps towards addiction are played out in the same circuits of the brain responsible for pleasure, relaxation and desire. These rely on substances with characteristics similar to opiates being produced in the brain, substances which are similar to the active agents in illegal drugs. These substances stimulate the brain's reward system creating a sense of well-being. All addictive substances trigger pleasurable sensations because the brain confuses them with the body's natural opioids. Some addictive substances stimulate the brain to release opioids and other neurotransmitters, even when nothing pleasant is going on externally. Drugs trick the pleasure system in this way and generate an artificial feeling of happiness.

Increasing Reliance

During the second phase of addiction those moments of pure pleasure gradually dwindle. Instead, cravings get the upper hand. Here, too, the responsible mechanisms are the brain's reward system and a particular neurotransmitter: dopamine, which generates a powerful desire for more. Addictive substances reinforce this vicious circle by causing dopamine levels to rise still higher. Anticipation can almost be as powerful as the drug itself: the very popping of the cork from a bottle of wine triggers a feeling of contentment, the sound of the lighter as a cigarette is lit, or the rustling of a sweet wrapper. The brain is slowly but surely reprogrammed.

WHAT IS SUGAR GOOD FOR?

As adults, we are all free to eat what we want, but recognizing our general dependency on sugar helps us to understand the choices we are making. And since, as we have seen, our systems are conditioned from birth to crave sweetness, we are going to have to reset some basic metabolic codes if we are going to be able to trust our senses and gut instincts. Perhaps the best way to begin this reset is by really appreciating and understanding how the body uses sugar and the dangers of over-consumption.

HOW THE BODY USES SUGAR

Sugar is one of our most important energy sources. It finds its way into the blood via the intestinal mucosa, where it forms blood sugar (blood glucose) and acts as an energy supplier to the rest of the body. But it may come as a surprise to discover that the most sugar-hungry part of the body is the brain.

EXCESS CONSUMPTION

Large sugar companies try to disassociate themselves from rising levels of obesity. They say the main cause for excess weight is an energy imbalance. This claim is basically correct. Anyone who eats more energy-giving food than the energy they use for physical activity (climbing stairs, walking, gardening and so on) will put on weight. And since our muscles use sugar as a source of energy, physical inactivity in combination with an excessive energy intake is the main reason today for being overweight.

A study in 2011 by the Organization for Economic Cooperation and Development (OECD) found half the population of its member states are too fat and noted that one in three children in the 33 OECD countries are overweight.

What's more: too much sugar doesn't just make you fat, it also makes you ill. It lowers life expectancy and increases the risk of cardiovascular disease, liver disease, type 2 diabetes, various types of cancer and a whole range of other difficult-to-treat illnesses.

We Are What We Eat

Sugar is not the only villain in this piece. Salt should
also be mentioned, as well as the additives and artificial
flavours that are employed to mask what we are really
eating. A strawberry yoghurt, for example, might be
coloured with beetroot or even wood chippings. Flavour
enhanced by sugar, fat and salt is cheaper to produce than
that of natural ingredients, so it always pays to read the
labels on the products that you buy with care.

The Role Played by Insulin

For our cells to be able to absorb and utilize sugar, they depend on
insulin. This hormone is produced in the pancreas and acts as a kind
of key. Insulin works by bonding to muscle, fat and the liver cells and
calling in the sugar. The faster the glucose gets into the intestine –
for example, after eating cakes and pastries or drinking fizzy drinks
– the higher the blood sugar levels rise and consequently insulin
concentration levels also rise. Ultimately the body tries to utilize the
sugar quickly to bring blood sugar levels down again.

Insulin also supports the brain's capacity for absorbing a certain
amino acid called tryptophan, which is essential to life and is found
in a variety of foods from meats to seeds and, interestingly, chocolate.
Tryptophan is converted in the brain into the mood-enhancing
hormone serotonin, which spontaneously lifts the spirits. If you're
stressed, in a bad mood, or lacking in energy, a handful of jelly babies
or an energy bar can offer you the double bonus of an energy boost
and a better mood.

Unfortunately neither of these effects is particularly long lasting.
The faster the blood sugar levels rise after a meal, the higher the
release of insulin and any positive effects are soon over.

NOT ALL SUGARS ARE THE SAME

Another type of sugar is starch. Initially, starch tastes of nothing at all and must first be transformed during the digestive process into glucose. You may only notice that this substance is actually sugar if, for instance, you chew well on a crust of bread and a sweet taste occurs. This is because the enzymes in our saliva break down the oligosaccharides (complex carbohydrates) in the crust into glucose.

Starch is found in many foodstuffs – in bread and pastries, pasta, rice and rice products, potatoes, corn and cereals. Sugar and starches are grouped together by nutritional scientists under the term 'carbohydrates'. Together with fats and proteins they form the three major nutrients in our diets.

STARCH AND THE METABOLISM

Depending on their chemical composition, carbohydrates can have a very different impact on blood sugar levels and on our overall metabolism. Glucose, in particular, acts as a vital energy supplier for the body. The brain, the red blood cells and the kidneys all need glucose to generate energy. This argument is used in many nutritional guidelines when dealing with high quantities of carbohydrates in our diet. Carbohydrates deliver readily available glucose. However, if our diet is low in carbohydrates, our metabolism can also generate glucose from protein and glycogen, so carbohydrates are not absolutely vital.

Until recently it was thought that the various kinds of sugar consumed in our diet were simply absorbed and broken down, or converted, into glucose so that the body could generate the required sugars it needed. However, it has become clear that the various different types of sugar actually have very varying negative or positive impacts on our health.

Sugars are not just a source of energy. They also play an important role in metabolism and in cell structure. Some of them are vital-signal carriers, acting as antennae for the immune system, and useful for the general calibration of the body as well as cellular repairs.

NATURAL SOURCES OF SUGAR

From a nutritionist's point of view, a diet based on fresh vegetables provides the ideal source of all types of sugar. Plants have all the essential substances we need – vitamins, minerals and dietary fibre.

Nowadays, many fruit and vegetable varieties are propagated for their sweet flavour – extra sweet pineapples and apples, for example. As a consequence, most of the varieties commonly found in our supermarkets today contain far lower quantities of certain vitamins and minerals than varieties that were available 30 years ago and that, to some extent, can still be found today in organic shops. Certain other nutrients are also lost by keeping foods for too long, through cooking and further processing such as preserving, canning or freezing.

HOW SUGAR GETS INTO PLANTS

Plants utilize the power of sunlight to convert carbon dioxide and water into simple sugars – so-called monosaccharides. This forms their natural energy reserve. These simple sugars are then transformed by the plant into a large number of further simple sugars, which can then be used to assemble complex information carriers (oligosaccharides and polysaccharides, see pages 22–3).

The quantity and complexity of sugars in fruits and plants include hemicellulose, cellulose, pectins, resins and mucus – all of them component parts of the materials that give plant cells their structure. More than 250 types of hemicellulose have been discovered alone. Hemicelluloses typically contain glucose and fructose, as well as the monosaccharides galactose, mannose, galacturonic acid and xylose – chief constituents of the diet of our forefathers and of many primitive peoples today. In the developed world we do not eat enough fresh fruit and vegetables, and so our diet contains too few free vegetal monosaccharides and oligosaccharides.

DIFFERENT SUGARS

Different sugars have a different impact on blood-sugar levels and on the release of insulin. With simple (monosaccharide) sugars, blood sugar can rise just ten minutes after consumption and the sugar is then quickly stowed away by insulin in our muscle and liver cells and, in case of surplus, in our fat cells. This results in us quickly being hungry for more. With long-chain sugars (the oligosaccharides and polysaccharides) the whole process happens more slowly.

SUGAR GROUP	SUGAR TYPE
Simple sugars (monosaccharides) Single sugar molecule. They form the building blocks for disaccharides and oligosaccharides.	**Glucose** (dextrose or grape sugar). At a basic level we obtain energy most quickly and effectively from glucose. If you compare your metabolism with an engine, glucose is like 'super petrol'. **Fructose** (fruit sugar) occurs naturally in honey and many fruits giving them their sweet taste. Fructose as a molecule is not to be confused with high-fructose corn syrup which is often used as a sweetening additive in processed food and drinks.
Double sugars (Disaccharides) Two monosaccharide molecules bonded together.	**Lactose** (milk sugar) has one molecule each of glucose and galactose. Many people, particularly adults, find lactose difficult to tolerate (lactose intolerance) because their bodies cannot produce the enzyme lactase which breaks down the milk sugar. **Maltose** (malt sugar) has two glucose molecules linked together. **Sucrose** (raw sugar or beet sugar) has one molecule each of glucose and fructose. Primarily used in the form of granulated sugar. **Isomaltulose** has, like sucrose, one molecule each of glucose and fructose, although here the molecules are joined differently. Isomaltulose occurs naturally in small quantities in honey and sugar-cane extract. After consumption blood sugar levels rise only very slowly.
Oligosaccharides Consists of between three and nine monosaccharide molecules. Primarily found in pulses and beans.	**Stachyose** has two galactose, one glucose and one fructose molecule. **Verbascose** has three galactose, one glucose and one fructose molecule.

SUGAR GROUP	SUGAR TYPE

Oligosaccharides

continued.

Trisaccharides are composed of three monosaccharides with two glycosidic bonds connecting them. Found in chickpeas, they are indigestible to humans, but act as a prebiotic, encouraging the growth of friendly bacteria in the intestine.

Polysaccharides

At least ten monosaccharide molecules.

Starch comes from cereals as well as rice, corn, potatoes and root vegetables and consists of long chains or tree-like branches of sugar structures. Unbranched starch causes blood sugar to rise slowly, whereas branched starch can trigger a faster rise than some monosaccharides and disaccharides.

Dextrin is formed when starch is broken down during digestion.

Inulin consists exclusively of fructose molecules. It is found in artichokes and parsnips.

Dietary fibre such as cellulose, hemicellulose, pectin and lignin are a part of the outer cell walls or the skin of fruits and vegetables. Whole grain products, therefore, contain lots of fibre. Dietary fibre aids the digestive system, makes us feel full more quickly, regulates blood fat and blood sugar values and forms a breeding ground for healthy intestinal flora.

Sugar replacements

Sugar replacements can be divided into sweeteners and sugar substitutes.

Sweeteners are based on either synthetic or natural compounds which taste very sweet. In contrast to household sugar and sugar substitutes, sweeteners have no or extremely minimal nutritional value and they protect tooth enamel. Despite this, the regular consumption of sweeteners can lead to an increase in the risk of heart attack or stroke and type 2 diabetes. They can also make you fat, because the body's sense of taste detects a sweet flavour and expects a correspondingly large amount of energy. The body learns then reacts wrongly to future sweet meals so that fewer calories are burned.

Sugar substitutes such as sorbitol, mannitol, isomalt, xylitol, maltitol and lactitol are carbohydrates that can be exploited without dependence on insulin. In large quantities, they can lead to flatulence and diarrhoea, because they are not completely absorbed by the small intestine.

GOOD AND BAD CARBOHYDRATES

When we refer to 'good' carbohydrates we mean those that cause a slow rise in blood sugar levels and consequently require the pancreas to release less insulin. Along with pure energy, 'good' or complex carbohydrates also contain vital vitamins and minerals as well as filling dietary fibre to help the digestive process. These also help to maintain blood sugar levels at a constant level for longer periods. The result is that we feel full for longer.

Simple, or 'bad' carbohydrates (such as sugary drinks and snacks, white rice, white bread, pastries, white pasta and potato) are digested more quickly, providing a quick rush of energy, but failing to fill you up and, worse, causing energy slumps soon after you have eaten.

THE GLYCAEMIC INDEX

To standardize comparisons of how carbohydrates influence blood sugar levels, we use the glycaemic index (GI). On a scale of 1 to 100 the increase in blood sugar content is measured against foods containing 50 g (2 oz) of carbohydrate.

Starchy foods such as rice or potatoes, that can be metabolized quickly, have the highest glycaemic index. These foods cause a far greater and more rapid rise in blood sugar levels than those with a low GI.

Low GI foods include many vegetables with a high water content. Tomatoes, for example, are slower to digest and the glucose contained in them is only slowly absorbed into the bloodstream. The glycaemic reaction is influenced by the type of sugar and starch in the food. Cooking and preparation methods as well as the proportions of other nutrients in the food, such as fat or protein, also have an impact on the glycaemic reaction.

The GI of cooked carrots is around 70. To ingest 50 g (2 oz) of carbohydrates you would need to consume around 700 g (1.5 lb) of carrots. A baguette also has a GI of 70. And yet just 100 g (4 oz) of baguette will supply you with 50 g (2 oz) of carbohydrate. Eating 100 g (4 oz) of white bread, therefore, results in the same blood sugar response as the consumption of 700 g (1.5 lb) of cooked carrots.

7 SIMPLE STEPS TO FREE YOURSELF FROM SUGAR DEPENDENCY

1. Know Your Sugars

Most of the sugar we consume is hidden: just because a food contains 'no added sugar', does not mean it has a low sugar content. Look out for sucrose, glucose, fructose, maltose, hydrolysed starch and invert sugar, corn syrup and even honey.

2. Log It

Keep a sugar diary of everything you eat each day, and when (which can be just as important). You may think you are not eating a lot of sugar, but you'll be surprised.

3. Be Realistic

The changes in your body will not happen overnight and it may take a few weeks to start to see the benefits. Don't be disappointed if you don't see immediate results, the plan is 12-weeks long to ensure your body adapts smoothly to a reduced sugar intake. You will notice a sure and steady improvement in your health as the days go by,

4. Ditch Fast Foods

Fast foods contain sugar – usually in the form of glutamates, which are flavour enhancers. The sweetness sends your internal insulin factory – the pancreas – into overdrive.

5. Switch to Healthy Sugars

Not all sugars are bad. There is sweetness in sweet potato, carrots and parsnips, and there are alternatives too (see pages 22–3).

6. Eat Fruit Early in the Day

Fresh fruit is high in vitamins, but contains fructose (natural fruit sugar), so take care to stick to single portions and eat it early in the day.

7. Get Moving

With activity, the body loses its reliance on excess sugar. Try following the exercise plans on pages 122–7.

7 BENEFITS OF GIVING UP SUGAR

1. Lose weight, feel great

By reducing your calorie intake you are helping your body work through
any excess stored in fat deposits, creating a leaner and healthier body.

2. Glowing skin

When substituting sugary snacks with fresh vegetables the body gets a
huge hit of vitamins, minerals and, most importantly, water. Blemishes
and dry patches are replaced with a brighter, healthier complexion.

3. Increased energy

Sugary snacks cause a quick 'high', but are soon followed by exhausting
energy slumps that leave you feeling more tired than you were before.
Managing the amount of sugar in your diet helps you feel brighter for longer.

4. Better digestion

Excess sugar consumption can cause extreme strain on the intestine and
it can contribute to sugar intolerance in irritable bowel syndrome sufferers.
Cutting back on sugar helps your intestine do its job as efficiently
as possible and can prevent bloating and other digestive problems.

5. Improved creativity and problem solving

Avoiding 'sugar highs' and the inevitable crashes thereafter results in
better concentration. Maintaining your energy levels throughout the day and
taking regular exercise also results in a better quality of sleep, which has endless
benefits in improving mental acuity.

6. Reduced anxiety

Sensible meal planning and paying careful attention to your body's needs help
establish comforting routines that prevent your mind and body becoming panicked
and craving snacks and fast food. A healthy body is a calmer body.

7. Save money

Preparing your own sugar-free snacks means pre-planning and sensible
shopping, which will reduce sneaky trips to the coffee shop and mean
spending less on expensive pre-prepared foods.

2

Sugar Science

Some scientists now consider sugar to be an addictive substance, and once hooked we constantly crave more. Find out what happens when sugar consumption goes beyond what is considered 'normal' and the potential risks involved. Discover the effect sugar has on the brain and what happens when a metabolic disorder develops, leading to insulin resistance and a host of related illnesses.

TOO MUCH SUGAR IS DANGEROUS

We are not talking about an occasional ice cream on a sunny day or a dessert to finish a meal. The real problem is the massive quantities of liquid or solid – pure or hidden – sugar that we are consuming all the time and that our bodies have become used to.

The power of habit only becomes apparent when you try to give something up. Your mood plummets with sugar deprivation and you experience depression, fatigue, irritability and a lack of concentration – all typical signs of low blood sugar levels and an altered brain chemistry that can only be put back on track by fuelling up fast with something sweet.

Consider what happens when we eat sweet things. The body cannot use sugar directly. To get the energy from the sugar the body needs insulin to convert it and this, in turn, supports cell division, growth, even basic body movements.

When a food is very rich in sugar, our blood sugar levels rise rapidly. The pancreas releases a large quantity of the key hormone insulin (see page 17). The consequence is that blood sugar levels plummet down again almost as rapidly as they rose. This drop in sugar results in gnawing feelings of hunger or food cravings. The faster the blood sugar level sinks, the stronger these cravings are.

But there is an imbalance here between what our brains tell us and what our bodies are saying. The brain is dependent on sugar. How full you feel after a meal has little to do with the energy content consumed in a meal. The more sugar and starch contained in a food, the more quickly we feel hungry again, even if our energy reserves are actually still pretty high.

An ideal diet of fresh fruits and vegetables, high-quality proteins, healthy sugars, sufficient liquid and appropriate breaks between meals will help protect the delicate equilibrium between blood sugar and insulin and reduce the strain on the pancreas.

INSULIN'S ADVERSARIES

As soon as blood sugar levels have been lowered again thanks to the release of the insulin, a further hormone called glucagon comes into play. This is released when there is too little sugar in the blood.

The Insulin-Glucagon Relationship

Normally insulin and glucagon work together to ensure that blood sugar values are maintained at levels between 80 to 180 mg of glucose per 100 ml of blood. To achieve this, glucagon bonds primarily with cells in the liver, where sugar chains in the form of glycogen are stored – glycogen is the body's natural way of storing glucose. The neurotransmitter then signals when the sugar chains should be dissolved in order to deliver glucose into the blood and at the same time ensures that new sugar is formed in the liver from protein building blocks. In this way the hormone guards against possible damage to the brain through hypoglycaemia (see page 33).

Glucagon also indirectly allows fat to break free and be converted into sugar. As a result, blood sugar levels and insulin levels rise again. Where food consumption is in line with levels of physical activity everything works well. But if the metabolism is knocked out of kilter over an extended period due to poor dietary habits – that is, too much sugar – then we have a vicious circle.

If these dietary habits are coupled with physical inactivity, then even less sugar and fat from food is burned and instead they end up deposited on the stomach, legs, bottom and in muscles, all of which gradually become fatter. In the worst cases, metabolic and obesity related illnesses arise. In the long term the incessant intake of glucose at frequent short intervals and the associated constant release of insulin also strain the pancreas.

METABOLIC SYNDROME

Insulin is essential for the correct functioning of the sugar metabolism and plays a role in the development of type 2 diabetes. Many decades after its discovery and commercial development in the 1920s and 1930s doctors, endocrinologists, molecular biologists and neuroscientists know far more about the way insulin works.

Poor Insulin Function

Until recently, it was thought that the principal consequences of a damaged insulin system were type 2 diabetes (that is, not congenital), cardiovascular disease and liver disease (fatty liver), as well as disturbances to our hormonal equilibrium. Today we know there are other consequences as well.

The upset of the finely balanced interplay of insulin and glucagon (see page 31) plays a significant role in the development of many other complaints. These include osteoporosis, hypertension, lipid metabolic disorders, renal failure, gout, myalgia, myasthenia, obesity, endocrine diseases like polycystic ovary syndrome (which can lead to infertility) and even a large number of cancers.

Brain-related Disorders

The insulin metabolism is also crucial in our understanding of illnesses of the brain, in particular Alzheimer's type dementia, since it plays a role in the functioning of the central nervous system.

Last, but now much more common, if the energy and sugar metabolisms are disrupted, we see stress-related illnesses and conditions like depression or burnout.

What is Hypoglycaemia?

The brain is very sensitive to low blood
sugar values (hypoglycaemia); symptoms include:

- tiredness
- delayed reaction times
- dizziness
- visual disturbances
- muscle cramps
- shivering
- weakness
- cravings for sweet, fatty or fast food
- inability to concentrate
- forgetfulness
- disorientation
- impatience, irritability
- dejection, depression

True hypoglycaemia, however, only occurs in
extreme sports or in diabetes sufferers, when blood
sugar values fall to 60 mg per 100 ml of blood. If
this occurs, the brain releases a cascade of stress
hormones such as adrenaline and cortisol.

Hypoglycaemia manifests itself in symptoms
such as breaking into a sweat, tachycardia (racing
heart) and nerviness. If blood sugar levels sink
even lower to around 40 mg per 100 ml the
consequence can be warped sensory perception and
slurred speech. The brain can no longer function
properly. In the worst case scenario this can be fatal.

INSULIN RESISTANCE

Insulin resistance is a condition where your body cannot deal properly with the amount of insulin it is producing, which can lead to type 2 diabetes and possibly heart disease.

STAGE 1: THE START OF INSULIN RESISTANCE

For any kind of movement, our muscles normally need energy extracted from food or from our body's fat stores. This only functions properly if intake and consumption are in harmony. If you spend most of the day sitting and/or you consume too many carbohydrates as well as saturated fatty acids – for example from meat or cheese – the body's natural feedback loop can be disrupted.

Eighty per cent of glucose absorbed is used by our muscles. With a constant intake of food, the system overheats, producing the damaging forms of oxygen that we call free radicals. In order to protect themselves against these processes, the muscle cells become insulin resistant, their doors remain firmly closed and any sugar continues to course through the bloodstream.

The body will try whatever it can to force the sugar into the cells and fix the backlog. The pancreas goes into overdrive and produces even more insulin. Any sugar that won't go into the cells, despite these efforts, simply ends up in the fat cells (adipocytes), which are almost infinitely expansible.

This is where energy should be stored for 'bad times', but because such times don't generally occur in a modern lifestyle, the fatty deposits just continue to grow. The fat cells become bloated and, as a result, the body may over-produce certain hormones which can then lead to illness or disease.

STAGE 2: PARTIAL INSULIN RESISTANCE

Without breaks between meals, and with insufficient physical activity, the body and the brain 'forget' what it means to eat normally. Eating habits can drift off into pathologically addictive behaviour – the body wants the energy it feels it is entitled to.

In the long term these hidden disturbances in the sugar metabolism will result in irreversible damage, but even in the early stages there can be a negative side, which can be detected in conventional blood tests. However, the compensatory release of increased amounts of insulin obscures these effects, so they can remain undetected for a long time.

Consequences of the Side Effects

- hypertension

- elevated levels of uric acid

- elevated levels of triglycerides (fat values)

- elevated cholesterol levels

- slightly elevated liver function readings

- slightly elevated urea levels

- utilization disturbances in the iron metabolism

- depleted iron levels

- depleted vitamin D levels

- bonding of the haemoglobin in red blood cells with
  an increase in HbA1C (see page 52)

STAGE 3: DERAILMENT OF THE SUGAR METABOLISM

If eating patterns continue unchanged, the metabolism can become completely derailed and instinctive feelings of hunger or satiation are permanently damaged.

The hormone leptin, which is thought to regulate hunger, was discovered in 1994. It is primarily emitted by fat cells (adipocytes), which use it to signal to the brain that they are replete. But the hormone is also produced by the pituitary gland and in the hypothalamus. It tells you, basically, that you have eaten enough. In someone who permanently eats too much sugar and fat, the neural centre in the brain which regulates appetite – the appestat – becomes used to the flood of leptin.

Due to this so-called leptin resistance, our appetite takes longer to curb. People keep on eating in spite of the leptin signals. And those affected generally also consume precisely that combination of nutrients that triggers particularly large releases of insulin and leptin: namely sugar and fat. Nowadays it is also recognized that insulin and leptin in the brain help orchestrate a whole range of processes connected with the intake of nutrients and indeed the natural compulsion to be physically active. An excess of these hormones makes us listless and apathetic. One possible mechanism that might aid self-regulation is therefore hindered.

A Weakened Immune System

In cases of insulin and leptin resistance, the availability and utilization of glucose is permanently damaged. Constantly elevated sugar values in the blood cause damage to numerous bodily structures. At the same time, the cells suffer from an inadequate supply of energy and building materials. The cells are unable to fulfil their role in the proper functioning of the metabolism and they are hardly able to regenerate themselves. This speeds up the ageing process and causes the immune system to be permanently weakened.

CONSEQUENCES OF INSULIN RESISTANCE

Pathologically elevated insulin values and insulin resistance lead to increases in abdominal fat and/or fat in the liver. This exacerbates hypertension, lipid metabolic disorders with high cholesterol and triglyceride values and vascular inflammation. Furthermore, the clotting system in the liver can be knocked off course.

The Liver-Brain Axis

As a result of the liver's clotting system not functioning properly, environmental toxins, carcinogenic nitrosamines, ammonia and high levels of the stress hormones CRH and cortisol can cross the liver-brain axis and trigger neurodegenerative and inflammatory processes in the brain. In this way, sugar can unleash a whole array of toxic consequences.

Metabolic disorders of the liver, which are closely associated with fatty liver disease, also greatly encourage insulin resistance in the brain. Learning processes, memory formation and concentration are permanently damaged.

The brain is impacted by the encroachment over the blood-brain barrier of toxic by-products and inflammatory substances, which can cause it severe damage.

Avoiding Insulin Resistance

The latest scientific research suggests that an imbalance in insulin levels and signs of insulin resistance should be detected and investigated as early as possible. If treated properly, these 'advance troops' signalling the various diseases that may follow can be intercepted and disarmed.

At the same time, the brain can be protected in the long term by taking diligent care of the liver, through an appropriate change in diet and a reduction in consumption of damaging sugars. This book aims to help you do just that.

SUGAR: THE BITTER TRUTH

One of the most prominent and engaged proponents of the theory that sugar is addictive is Professor Robert H Lustig, a paediatrician at the University of California, San Francisco. In a 2009 lecture that he gave, entitled 'Sugar: The Bitter Truth' he illustrated how close the relationship between sugar and the brain really is. The lecture has received over 5 million hits on YouTube to date.

LUSTIG'S THEORY

It all begins with a substance dependency and this is the same for everyone, because it is rooted in our biological blueprint: almost every organ in the body is dependent on insulin for its supply of blood glucose. Only nerve cells can absorb glucose without recourse to insulin. For this process to occur it doesn't matter if you eat a bag of sweets, an apple, or a piece of salmon, because the bodies can convert starch, fat and protein into glucose, which is then transmitted via our bloodstream into the brain.

If necessary, muscle cells can also burn fat as soon as sugar stores are depleted. That happens, for example, at night when we are asleep and so inevitably experience an extended period without food.

The brain, on the other hand, is unable to extract energy from fat. The most direct supply of energy for our grey matter is from pure glucose. If a torrent of blood sugar and insulin is triggered by constant overconsumption of sugar, the result is not just permanent food cravings, but also physical signs of addictive changes in the brain's metabolism. Until relatively recently many experts were still convinced that foodstuffs were fundamentally not addictive. The question is still hotly debated, but more recent studies demonstrate all kinds of parallels between intoxicants.

ARE YOU A SUGAR JUNKIE?

Professor Achim Peters, a doctor from Lübeck, Germany, has identified that it is the sugar status in our brains rather than our blood sugar levels in general that determine whether we develop an appetite for particular nutrients, especially carbohydrates.

THE ROLE YOUR BRAIN PLAYS

In order to guarantee its supply of sugar, the brain is equipped with various energy control modules. These consist of a network of neurons that originate in the uppermost hierarchical regions of the brain, then pass over into the brain stem and from there travel out through the body to the liver, pancreas and finally to the muscles.

If necessary our brain cells can also simply extract glucose from the blood. The evidence for this kind of system is based on pathological research carried by Marie Krieger in 1921. Looking at malnutrition in young soldiers who died during the First World War, she established that under conditions of starvation (and therefore sugar deprivation) the internal organs shrink by up to 40 per cent. The one exception to this is the brain, which at most loses two per cent of its overall mass.

So, although the brain only accounts for two per cent of the body's weight in terms of its mass, it requires a good half of the daily intake of carbohydrates. In normal conditions it may consume two-thirds of blood glucose quantities. Put under stress, our grey matter can take up to 90 per cent of these valuable energy sources.

Retraining the Brain

Reprogramming your metabolism is possible. We know that the liver can produce glucose itself from fats and amino acids and so is not dependent on an external supply of sugar and carbohydrates. If there is a stark reduction in the supply of carbohydrates and sugar, the brain can actually generate its own super fuel in the form of substances called ketone bodies. They are only produced by the body's liver fat metabolism when blood sugar levels are low and they act as a quickly obtainable energy supply for sugar dependent organs like the brain.

Warning Signs of Addiction

Frequent cravings for sweet things, snacking between meals, a longing for fruit juices or sweet drinks, an excessive predilection for bread, noodles and pasta or pizza as well as high fruit consumption in the evening should be enough to make us prick up our ears and consider whether or not we have developed an addiction. This is particularly the case if we feel tired and less able to concentrate after a meal.

There are several additional indicators, as follows:

- mood swings and 'energy crises'
- pressure or a feeling of tension in the abdomen
- difficulty in sleeping
- a state of anxiety, tension after eating
- particular cravings for dairy or starch

HOW BRAIN CHEMISTRY
IS TRICKED

The feeling of a 'high' that arises after the consumption of addictive substances originates in the *nucleus accumbens*, a region in the forefront of the brain, where the brain's so-called reward system is also located. Just like taking morphine, heroin or cannabis, consuming sugar causes, via the taste buds, the release (admittedly in smaller quantities) of opioids, and also the neurotransmitter dopamine.

This happiness hormone drives us to repeat pleasurable experiences again as soon as possible and to avoid negative ones. Sweet things belong to those experiences that the brain registers as pleasurable, just like, for example, sex, success or affection.

A further hormone, the mood-enhancing neurotransmitter serotonin, ensures that we evaluate sugar as a positive thing. Serotonin is normally produced under the influence of sunlight and makes us alert and capable. People who suffer from depression often exhibit a lack of serotonin. For people who are depressed or stressed, sugar is often their closest ally to help cheer them up again. This is because sugar in a meal also triggers the release of serotonin in the brain.

ABOUT DOPAMINE

Dopamine acts as a vital driving force behind every kind of self-destructive addictive behaviour. The high you get after taking drugs, the joy, pleasure and confidence you experience from the things you cherish, or from going for a run – all these can be traced back to an increased release of dopamine. The brain's reward system is responsible for this and we can stimulate it ourselves.

Concentrations of dopamine in the brain are at their highest when we are craving a particular stimulus or substance. Typically the highest dopamine peaks occur while we are still contemplating the imminent experience of something pleasurable or before the real-life execution of an intoxicating deed. Then we develop a true craving for the desired item. If you get what you want, dopamine levels sink again, and you crave even more.

A meal's primary impact is its taste, rather than its calories or its size, which expands the stomach and so sends the appropriate signal that we are replete. With advanced sugar addiction even just the packaging or an aroma can act as a suggestive prompt that stimulates dopamine production. This steers us towards eating something that will then trigger a release of opioids. The positive experience we get from the connection between these substances encourages us to keep eating.

How to Boost Dopamine Naturally

Evidence of a dopamine shortfall manifests itself through chronic fatigue syndrome, muscular weakness, concentration disorders, forgetfulness, attention deficits, daytime sleepiness, apathy and also restless-leg syndrome. Because dopamine is formed from the amino acid tyrosine, steps can be taken to increase the body's tyrosine levels with a protein-rich diet; in particular fish, lean meat, milk, eggs and also wholemeal products, nuts and peas. With the assistance of vitamins B6 and B12 as well as magnesium, dopamine can be generated and stored in our neurons without a dependency on insulin.

ABOUT SEROTONIN

Serotonin is primarily responsible for good spirits. If serotonin levels are sufficiently high, our spirits rise and we feel optimistic, content and relaxed and we sleep soundly at night. It is at night-time that serotonin is converted into the sleep hormone melatonin.

Low serotonin values can result in poor sleep, poor concentration, falling productivity, anxiety, aggression, difficulty making decisions, depressive resentment or increased appetite. In addition, loss of libido, sensitivity to pain and migraines are all influenced by serotonin. The lower our serotonin values, the greater the probability of developing an addiction. Serotonin is present in various foodstuffs in the form of the amino acid tryptophan. Large quantities are present, for example, in certain fruits and vegetables like kiwis, bananas, pineapple and tomatoes.

ABOUT TRYPTOPHAN

Tryptophan cannot cross the blood-brain barrier, whereas sugar from food can. It triggers a series of intermediary processes that stimulate production of serotonin in the brain. Normally tryptophan continues to circulate in the bloodstream until other essential amino acids are channelled across the blood-brain barrier. Only when we eat something sweet can tryptophan briefly conquer these rivals and secure itself an appropriate mode of transport. This works best with a combination of fat and sugar. And this is precisely why many people suffering from a serotonin deficiency crave carbohydrates.

How does it work?

The sugar boosts the production of insulin in the pancreas. And this insulin doesn't just ship glucose to its required destination, but also other nutrients which act as cell building blocks. The insulin channels the aforementioned amino acids into the cell's interior. Tryptophan can now flow unrivalled through the blood and from there into the brain where it is converted into serotonin.

Anyone who has made this connection either consciously or unconsciously, perhaps in a glass of warm milk and honey in the evening, or a bar of chocolate to see them through the post-lunch slump, will then automatically reach for something sweet as soon as they feel stressed, can't relax or are unable to sleep.

Unfortunately the mechanism has a short-term effect, and then only in healthy people. With excessive sugar and carbohydrate consumption there follows a second phase in which levels of tryptophan, B vitamins and amino acids in the blood fall again. On the one hand this is due to insulin resistance. And on the other hand an excess consumption of sugar and carbohydrates acts directly in a negative way on serotonin levels. A vicious circle begins: too much sugar inhibits the feel good hormone serotonin, and the subsequent feeling of malaise results in a greater craving for carbohydrates and sugar. Even a small serotonin deficiency can result in a proper case of the 'snack attacks'.

LEARNING TO DO
WITHOUT SUGAR

Someone who has spent years eating predominantly highly processed foods may only realise they've become dependent on them when they try to convert to a 'healthy' diet. Some scientists have even suggested that the symptoms of withdrawal from crisps, sweeteners, soft drinks and ready meals are strikingly similar to those experiencing withdrawal from heroin or cocaine.

If properly recognized and treated individually, many of the metabolic disorders described in the previous pages are eminently curable. Nutrition constitutes a central pillar of treatment and prevention. Unfortunately it is not a simple case of just turning off the 'sugar tap' from one day to the next. If you go cold turkey, your so-called stress response system will leap panic stricken into action. Dopamine production levels will sink through the floor. In exceptional circumstances the stress hormones may be thrown out of kilter in the longer term. Although the withdrawal symptoms only last for around a week, you remain at greater risk of resorting to sugar in order to calm yourself down in any future situations associated with stress. This is how relapses occur.

Activity, sport, acupuncture and sensitive changes to diet can all help in a variety of ways. In particular, by using the sugar substitute galactose, withdrawal symptoms and relapses can be intercepted and overcome. This healthy sugar helps avoid sweet cravings, without having an effect on the insulin metabolism. Even an existing case of insulin resistance can be overcome by reducing the intake of 'bad' carbohydrates in the form of industrialized sugar, and instead converting to healthy sugars and a generally fresh diet high in essential nutrients.

Taking this approach makes the muscle cells more sensitive to insulin again and means they can be supplied with sufficient nutrients. Our internal systems will run smoothly once more.

3

How Sugar
Makes You Ill

*If you think that a diet high in sugar
simply makes people gain weight, think again.
There are numerous illnesses associated
with sugar addiction, not least type 2 diabetes,
hypertension, cancer and ADHD.
Discover the measures that you can take
in order to alleviate symptoms and/or
to prevent them altogether.*

SYMPTOMS OF EXCESS SUGAR INTAKE

People don't normally get sick completely out of the blue. Illness is usually preceded by a number of negative contributory factors, which together compromise our immune systems and reveal themselves in various physical symptoms and psychological imbalances.

Nowadays we know that a myriad of conditions and chronic illnesses are related to diet. Sugar in particular is contributing to illness in an insidious manner either in combination with other substances or on its own as an essential ingredient in highly processed industrialized foods. The first signs are often ever more frequently recurring classic hypoglycaemic symptoms after the consumption of sugar-rich meals, soft drinks or snacks, which in theory should be giving you a lift after an energy dip, or alleviating your frustration, boredom or stress. Over time your metabolism goes off the rails due to a continual overconsumption of sugar, and this paves the way for various conditions that conventional medicine regards as difficult or impossible to cure.

SECRET KILLER

Until a few years ago, type 2 diabetes was the only officially recognized 'sugar sickness', but nowadays nutritional doctors and scientists know that, as a result of the modern sugar-rich diet, the pancreas and the liver, the kidneys, muscles and skeleton as well as blood vessels (and therefore the cardiovascular system) are all affected by any malfunctioning in our central sugar and insulin metabolisms.

Many of the damaging effects of simple carbohydrates and bad sugars, however, can remain undetected in the body. Since blood sugar levels can appear normal over long periods of time, a doctor just considering this indicator may not see the damage and deterioration taking part in other parts of the body.

For instance, low iron and/or ferritin levels, fatigue, thyroid conditions, insomnia, chronic pain and psychological well-being are often not connected with an impaired sugar metabolism and, as such, are treated as isolated conditions. Unfortunately this is often with little success: iron supplements, sedatives and pain medication as well as antidepressants are often short-term and unsustainable solutions.

Even worse, the damaging causes behind these conditions remain undetected and can continue to cause more widespread damage to the body. Vital years where early intervention might have been possible are missed in this way. The facts and figures for the mechanisms behind this damage have been known for a long time. Despite this, there is often a failure to take a holistic view and make these connections.

Why Sugar is So Dangerous

Every high-carbohydrate meal of bread, pasta, pizza, cake, fruit juices and soft drinks results in high blood sugar levels (hyperglycaemia). This triggers the release of insulin. Too many carbohydrates consumed too often and in high concentrations results in a permanently elevated and excessive release of insulin in order to keep blood sugar levels within normal healthy limits.

BLOOD SUGAR MEMORY

A particular measured blood sugar value is only ever really a snapshot in time. The value will vary depending on what you have eaten or drunk beforehand or how much exercise you've had. Stress levels, infection, temperature, hormonal variations and your condition on the day all influence the value too.

If you want to know how your blood sugar levels are behaving over a longer time frame, then your doctor will have to undertake a blood analysis to investigate the so-called HbA1c value. This is also known as your 'blood sugar memory' and represents your blood sugar levels over several weeks.

The basis of the HbA1c value are sugar particles, which accumulate in the red haemoglobin (Hb) within the red blood cells. This haemoglobin adorned with a 'sugar coating' is known as glycated haemoglobin (HbA1). The majority of the sugar coating clings to a subunit of the haemoglobin, the HbA1c.

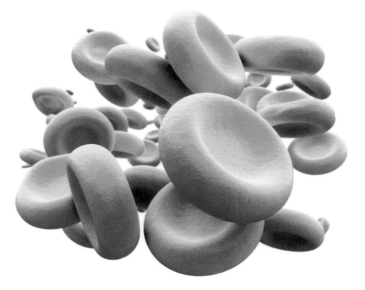

WHEN IS FAT TOO FAT?

Obesity is one of the main risk factors for type 2 diabetes, as well as for high blood pressure, disorders of the fat metabolism and other vascular diseases.

These conditions together form what is sometimes described as metabolic syndrome – also known as syndrome X or insulin-resistance syndrome (see pages 34–8). They can occur at any age, even in small children and young adults.

Metabolic syndrome (see page 32) is not a discrete illness. In fact, it is a whole collection of particular symptoms, which can increase the risk of arteriosclerosis, along with other vascular complaints and cardiovascular disease. It is also connected with an increased risk of various types of cancer, hormonal disorders, alimentary tract diseases as well as degenerative diseases of the musculoskeletal system. Obesity in middle-age has also been implicated in the onset of dementia, and particularly Alzheimer's.

We are all aware of the health implications of being overweight, and yet the problem is widespread and continues to grow. One argument for this is that we find it difficult to judge what our healthy weight should be, given that human bodies vary dramatically in height and muscle mass. This is why doctors use the Body Mass Index (BMI) to assess body weight and potential risk factors to health.

How to Measure Your BMI

To ascertain your BMI divide your weight (in kilograms) by your height (in metres), then divide the result by your height again to find your BMI. (For example, if you weigh 70 kg and you're 1.75 m tall, divide 70 by 1.75, which is 40. Then divide 40 by 1.75 to reach a BMI of 22.9.) If your BMI is under 18 you may well be underweight, and if it is 30 or over, you are clinically obese.

DANGEROUS ABDOMINAL FAT

The fatty tissue in the stomach (visceral fat) is not necessarily noticeable in people with the classic 'apple'-shaped body. But even apparently slim people can have a high proportion of abdominal fat. The fat is initially laid down on the internal organs, before it becomes noticeable in the form of a spare tyre. Fat in the liver is particularly risky to our health.

In excess, this abdominal fat acts as an independent hormone system, since the fat cells (adipocytes) produce a whole array of new signals and messages that interfere with the immune system.

For example:

- More leptin (the hunger-regulating hormone) is produced, upsetting appetite and eating habits;
- But the toxins also make us hungry and want to eat more;
- And as the body develops an insulin resistance, the muscles get lazy, so we put on weight.

In turn this calls in the stress hormone cortisol, which further inhibits the insulin and causes more glucose to course through our veins.

How to Measure Your Waist

Ideally you should measure your waist first thing in the morning before breakfast. Stand in front of a mirror to check that you are standing up straight. Lay the tape measure at navel height and take it once around your body. Breath out gently. It is easiest to read the result with the tape measure placed upside down. Health risks increase once a woman's abdominal circumference is greater than 80 cm and a man's greater than 88 cm. The NHS recommends that women should have a maximum waist of 88 cm and men no more than 102 cm.

FACTORS AFFECTING BODY WEIGHT

1. Bad Eating Habits

This involves an intake of too many of the wrong nutrients:
high-energy, high-sugar and high-fat food products. Frequent
snacking, fast food, sugar-laden soft drinks and alcoholic drinks
don't fill you up but instead make you hungrier. The calorie content
of meals is a secondary issue. It's not excessive quantities that make
you fat, but ultimately an impaired metabolism. Only one-fifth
of overweight people have tipped the scales towards obesity simply
as a result of the desire to overeat. Your weight only remains stable if
the energy derived from your food corresponds to the amount
of energy being used by your body.

2. Hormonal Issues

An underactive thyroid, or Cushing's syndrome, in which the
level of the stress hormone cortisol is permanently elevated,
can also play a role in obesity. Hormonal fluctuations, particularly
in girls during puberty and in women during pregnancy or during the
menopause can also facilitate rapid weight gains. But the hormonal
metabolism can equally be derailed by taking certain medications,
such as antidepressants or antidiabetics, beta blockers,
glucocorticosteroids and neuroleptics.

3. Genetic Predisposition

It is speculated that body weight is about 60–80 per cent
attributable to genetic factors. Nevertheless there are certain
environmental factors responsible for a hereditary illness.
We should not overlook psychological factors such as stress,
loneliness or frustration which can lead to incessant eating.
Negative feelings or discomfort are then misinterpreted as
hunger or appetite (for something sweet).

OBESITY AND CANCER

Obesity will soon overtake smoking as the prime cause of most common cancers. Even if you are just a little over a healthy weight there is an increased risk of developing cancer. Studies have proven that elevated levels of circulating insulin and IGF (insulin growth factor) in the blood are linked to an increased risk of cancer and Cancer Research UK note that more than 1 in 20 cancers in the UK are now linked to being overweight or obese (including cancer of the oesophagus, breast, liver, pancreas, kidney, bowel, womb, gallbladder, prostate and ovaries).

From a biological point of view, humans are perfect energy-saving machines. When we eat too much, this is immediately laid down in fat deposits on our stomach, legs and bottom. It is possible to lose weight sustainably and for the long term but it requires a sensible and calm approach. Changes won't happen overnight, but with sensible dietary changes progress can be made.

And although a reduction in food consumption is always desirable, there is no getting around the issue of regular physical activity. Since skeletal muscles consume 80 per cent of glucose it is important not to lose muscle mass. For a healthy synergy between muscles and bones you could also try walking up stairs. Just climbing 50 steps a day helps stabilize your bones.

Lactose in Milk

Milk and milk products from mammals contain a natural sugar called lactose. Usually a 235-ml glass of cow's milk will contain approximately 12 g of sugar and opting for a low-fat version won't necessarily change the sugar content. Goat's milk still contains some lactose, although less than cow's milk. The recipes in this book use lactose-free milk, which was developed for people with a lactose intolerance but is now widely available.

ARTERIOSCLEROSIS

Blood vessels are flexible and highly resilient, they expand and contract as necessary and operate over a network of around 100,000 km (62,140 miles) providing a perfect mode of transport and effective supplier for all the organs and cells in the body. Each individual blood vessel is reinforced by ring-shaped outer, middle and inner muscle layers. In conjunction with the smooth vessel walls (endothelium) this guarantees optimal flow conditions. The thickening and hardening of the walls of the arteries, occurring typically in old age, is known as arteriosclerosis. However with a balanced diet and healthy lifestyle the system can remain adaptable and efficient well into later life.

A LOSS OF ELASTICITY

Constricted and irritably inflamed blood vessels in any part of the body can result in vascular calcification and arteriosclerosis. The principle culprits of this are sugar and fats in our food: white flour, household and fruit sugars as well as simple carbohydrates are transformed into toxic fat. Excess fat, high triglyceride levels and an elevated cholesterol level are consequences of overloading the body with sugar and carbohydrates. Cholesterol in food, for example as consumed in eggs, is no longer thought to be the root cause, although it was frowned upon for a long time. Far more dangerous is the oxidized cholesterol in the liver that is converted from sugar.

Normally this kind of arteriosclerosis is a late complication of type 2 diabetes, but the onset of the vascular condition occurs decades before a diabetes diagnosis and the vascular system also comes under pressure in the early stages of metabolic syndrome.

A NATURAL APPROACH

A calorie-reduced diet, fewer carbohydrates, fewer hydrogenated fats and trans-fatty acids (artificial fats that the human body can't generate itself), less sugar and fewer soft drinks and, instead, more vegetables, fruits low in glucose and fructose, saltwater fish, (organic) meat, fresh herbs and pulses can offer far-reaching help and prevention of vascular calcification. Trans-fatty acids are particularly unhealthy. They considerably increase the risk of cardiac disease and diabetes. They are found in highly processed foods such as baked goods; confectionery; fried meals and snacks; frozen food; and margarine.

Natural protection for the whole vascular system can be offered by a range of unsaturated fatty acids, in particular the valuable omega-3 fatty acids, the amino acids arginine, methionine and cysteine, the minerals magnesium, zinc, selenium and chromium as well as sensible combinations of Vitamin C, E, B and D.

There is also evidence that a variety of natural substances and so-called secondary plant compounds can have a positive effect on heart, circulation, vascular and neurological protection – Ginkgo biloba, quince, rice bran, lecithin, ginger, black pepper, milk thistle, hawthorn and garlic are just a few with significant potential health benefits.

DIGESTIVE PROBLEMS

A relatively new widespread disease resides in the gut – so-called irritable bowel syndrome (IBS). Those affected suffer from bloating, cramps, diarrhoea or also constipation. The most common cause is that your bowel is fighting back against certain items in your diet.

Even Hippocrates recognized that all health is dependent on your intestine. Traditional healing systems from the Asian region, like Ayurveda or traditional Chinese medicine, lay particular emphasis on the health of the intestine and, as a result of this, on nutrition.

The gastro-intestinal system is enveloped by its own nervous system comprising about 100 million cells. This so-called enteric nervous system is, like the brain, highly complex, for which reason it is also referred to as the 'belly brain'.

Many researchers treat the belly brain like a copy of the true brain. Cell types and docking sites on the somatic cells (receptors) in the gastro-intestinal tract are, for instance, identical to those in the brain's control centre and they communicate with each other by means of their own neurotransmitters like, for example, serotonin or dopamine.

There is also a direct link via certain nerve pathways into the cerebrum and into the limbic system, that area of the brain in which all our urges and feelings originate. Everyone has experienced that sickening feeling in your stomach, which is evidence that your body reacts sooner than your consciousness.

STRAINS ON THE INTESTINE

Lactose (milk sugar) can cause an extreme strain on the intestine. Sufferers cannot break down the milk sugar because, in their intestine, the enzyme responsible for this process (lactase) is present in too small quantities or is not generated at all. The undigested lactose spreads into the deepest regions of the intestine where it leads to stomach aches, bloating and diarrhoea.

Fruit sugar (fructose) is absorbed from the cells of the small intestine by means of a special transporter mechanism (GLUT5) and thus channelled into the blood circulation system. If these processes fail, then fructose intolerance or so-called fructose malabsorption can occur. The incompletely processed fructose in the small intestine then ends up to a great extent in the large intestine and is consumed and fermented there by intestinal bacteria. If there is always a sufficient supply of fructose, certain intestinal bacteria will multiply and exacerbate any digestive problems.

At some point, the intestine stretches to such an extent as a result of bloating, that the mucosal fold between small and large intestine can no longer close properly. The contents of the large intestine, with its specific bacterial cultures, flow into the small intestine, in which other bacteria reside. The small intestine reacts to the invasion of these unwanted guests by becoming inflamed.

SUGAR INTOLERANCE AND IBS

Around 20 to 40 per cent of IBS sufferers appear to suffer from sugar intolerance. Fructose and sorbitol are especially in the spotlight here. Fructose in particular is a very common ingredient in highly processed foods in the form of corn syrup. The artificial sugar sorbitol (E420, also known as glucitol) is similarly a frequent addition to convenience foods.

Anyone who suffers from IBS or other forms of sugar intolerance will not find it easy to avoid consuming the offending food. Particularly the problematic sugars like milk sugar (lactose) and fruit sugar (fructose) which are found in nearly all processed foods.

Lactose, which stems from over production in the European milk industry, serves as a cheap flavour enhancer and stabilizing agent. The same applies to whey, which is a 'waste product' of cheese production and is cheap and high in lactose. Even fructose (particularly from corn) is almost omnipresent. It is also becoming more and more common for products to contain fructose-glucose syrup, a sugar concentrate that is extracted from cornstarch and passes particularly quickly into our blood.

HYPERTENSION

In the past two decades ever-increasing numbers of people have developed high blood pressure as a chronic condition (hypertension) or as a symptom of other metabolic conditions (see page 32). Today one in five of the western European population is affected. A shockingly high number when you consider that high blood pressure in the long term leads to arteriosclerosis, and so raises the risk of other cardiovascular illnesses, including heart attack.

WHAT IS HYPERTENSION?

Hypertension is identified when systolic blood pressure (the phase during which the heart contracts and blood is pumped out) is over 140mmHg and diastolic blood pressure (the phase during which the heart muscle relaxes and expands and blood flows in) is over 90mmHg.

Why a Rise in Blood Pressure?

Nutritional deficiencies are the main contributors responsible for high blood pressure. For a long time, the main focus of scientific research was excess salt consumption. More recently, it appears that the prime culprit is, in fact, sugar.

Fructose, in particular, seems to be chiefly responsible for vascular disease and hypertension. This was established in 2010 by researchers from the University of Colorado Denver Health Center. They concluded that the increase in the number of people suffering from high blood pressure is particularly closely related to the fact that in the last 20 years highly processed foods have been increasingly sweetened with cheap fruit sugars.

This is particularly significant for diabetics as their diet products are often high in added fructose, which can be absorbed by the body without the aid of insulin. The researchers, led by Diana Jalal, established that people who consumed more than 74 g (2.5 oz) of fructose – for example in the form of two and a half glasses of lemonade or apple juice – showed blood pressure levels that were between 26–77 per cent higher than the normal value of 80mmHg.

Hypertension and Insulin Resistance

At least half of all patients with high blood pressure suffer from insulin resistance. Insulin resistance causes less nitrogen monoxide to be produced and the blood vessels become too small. Inflammatory neurotransmitters get the upper hand and trigger vascular damage.

Easing the Strain

If you are a smoker and suffer from high blood pressure, the first measure to ease the strain on your vascular system is to give up nicotine. Regular exercise is also helpful and serves to rejuvenate the blood vessels. Physical exercise can generate nitrogen monoxide. This improves cell supply and can even reduce vascular deposits and seal up lesions in the walls.

The third contributor to vascular protection is nutrition. Lose weight with a long-term balanced diet. Fat cells are inflammatory cells. What's more, weight loss will help your body to become more sensitive to insulin again and any insulin resistance will abate. Amongst other things, meals should be put together so that they are rich in vascular-protecting food stuffs, above all omega-3 fatty acids. The body incorporates these into the inner vascular walls and this makes them more flexible.

DEPRESSION

Ever more people nowadays complain of symptoms ranging from sleeplessness, low mood and discontentment right up to full-blown depression. It is far less common than is generally assumed for psychological problems to be the root cause of such mental-health imbalances. Instead there is increasing reference to the connection between nutrition and mental well-being.

Given the marked escalation in such symptoms over the last 10 to 20 years, it is surely worth speculating about the extent to which this may be linked with lifestyle. The most obvious lifestyle changes in that time are an increased consumption of sugar and a lack of physical activity.

A 50- to 60-hour week was the norm 40 years ago, but was not a cause of extreme exhaustion. The ever-increasing complexity of the world may present excessive demands. When this is accompanied by stress, the combined effects of the hormones adrenaline, cortisol and insulin, the disruption of circadian rhythms, bad eating habits and physical inactivity, it is not hard to imagine why this must culminate in the destabilization of our metabolic equilibrium.

FRUCTOSE INTOLERANCE

Austrian nutritional expert Maximilian Ledochowski demonstrated a connection between fructose intolerance and depression in 2001. He found that fructose influences the metabolization of amino acids. When someone is fructose intolerant tryptophan (see page 17) can no longer be absorbed from the intestine. This occurs because the fructose bonds with the tryptophan and carries it through into the large intestine. So the tryptophan fails to be conveyed as normal from the small intestine into the brain via the blood stream, where it is needed as the most important building block for the 'happiness hormone' serotonin. If the amino acid is lacking, serotonin cannot be generated. In the case of a prevailing insulin resistance, however, it is not just serotonin synthesis that is restricted. Serotonin transporters and receptors also become less sensitive. The effective levels and impact of the remaining serotonin actually fall. And with that the person's mood falls through the floor.

Stress Makes you Ill

In patients with depression the stress hormone cortisol is elevated and insulin resistance is increased. Chronic stress, nutritional stress, excess release of cortisol along with its controlling hormone CRH and elevated insulin levels alter the biochemical decisions in the metabolism of depression. Many experts today agree that too much stress leads to depression and that people suffering from depression experience particularly high stress levels. Elevated levels of CRH, cortisol and insulin as well as a pre-existing insulin resistance simultaneously reduce the availability of the calming neurotransmitter serotonin. Low serotonin levels are then an additional cause of anxiety and depression.

ELEVATED INSULIN LEVELS

Today's eating habits involve incessant consumption. People live in a perpetually sated state and, therefore, under constant oxidative stress. Our insulin levels are permanently elevated. This not only means that physiological stress reduction is hampered, but also circadian rhythms are disturbed. Elevated insulin levels in the evening and at night hinder the production of growth hormones as well as serotonin and the sleep hormone melatonin. Possible consequences are bad moods, anxiety, increased sensitivity to pain, poor sleep and depression.

You can combat such imbalances in particular with a low-sugar diet. Take special care not to consume any carbohydrates in the evening. A switch to healthy sugar is recommended in any case. This can be supported by consuming foods that are high in antioxidants (such as blueberries) as well as taking regular exercise in the fresh air as exposure to sunlight can further stimulate the production of serotonin.

TYPE 2 DIABETES

If you continuously supply the body with too much sugar through
your diet, your blood sugar levels will be constantly elevated and
the cells soon full to the brim with sugar. You no longer respond to
insulin, which would normally signal to the cells to take up the sugar.
Instead you become insulin resistant. The consequence is that the sugar
remains in the blood. The pancreas releases still more insulin to try to
force the sugar into the cells, until at some point it gives up. The sugar
metabolism goes into complete collapse and the result is diabetes.

DIFFERENT FORMS OF DIABETES.

There are two forms of diabetes, known as type 1 and type 2.

- Type 1 diabetes relates to an autoimmune disease that usually
  begins in childhood or adolescence and is also known as 'juvenile
  diabetes'. Because the insulin-generating beta cells are destroyed
  by the body's own antibodies, the pancreas is unable to produce
  the hormone and the patient suffers from insulin deficiency. Type
  1 diabetics must, therefore, inject themselves with insulin for their
  whole lives. The causes of type 1 diabetes are a combination of an
  inherited predisposition and external factors (for example certain
  viral infections) as well as a malfunctioning of the immune system.
  Diet and high sugar consumption play no role here.

- With type 2 diabetes the symptoms develop slowly over several
  years. Warning signals may be noticed during this preliminary
  stage (see box, page 70), but the link between these conditions and
  diabetic illness is often not made. The condition can therefore remain
  undetected for some time. Frequently it is secondary illnesses such as
  cardiovascular complaints, kidney ailments, eye diseases that point to
  the metabolic disorder.

Type 2 diabetes can occur at any age and is primarily caused by
environmental factors and lifestyle. With increasing blood sugar, the
beta cells in the pancreas cease to function properly and the sensitivity

Gestational Diabetes

During pregnancy normal blood sugar levels are particularly important, since levels which are too high or indeed too low can damage the embryo. If dietary change cannot produce an effective result, gestational diabetes, like other forms of diabetes, is treated with insulin.

of receptors and glucose transporters is impaired. Over the years this causes the fasting blood sugar level to continue to rise until it reaches a value of over 110 mg/dl (over 180 mg/ml two hours after a meal).

ELEVATED BLOOD SUGAR LEVELS?

The main contributors to a malfunctioning sugar metabolism are obesity, physical inactivity and a diet that is too high in fat and sugar. This has been confirmed in animal research. A group of mice were given fatty foods along with carbohydrates; a control group were just given fatty foods without the carbohydrates. Both groups put on weight and, after 17 weeks, were equally overweight. Most mice in the first group were exhibiting elevated blood sugar levels after just 8 weeks. By the seventeenth week around two-thirds of the animals from this first group were suffering from diabetes. The animals in the second group were not affected. As research on the beta cells in the pancreas eventually showed, ingested carbohydrates influence the activation of 39 genes, which, in humans, are connected with developing diabetes.

Scientists at the German Institute for Nutritional Research in Potsdam-Rehbrück also showed in animal research that carbohydrate damages the insulin-producing cells in the pancreas. In combination with nutritional fats, the oxidative stress in the cells is increased which results in accelerated cell ageing and cell death. Furthermore, scientists from the Max Planck Institute established that the happiness hormone serotonin also plays an important role in the development of diabetes. They claim that a shortage of this neurotransmitter in the

Telltale Signs of Diabetes

According to the International Diabetes Federation,
1 in 12 of the world's population suffers from diabetes
mellitus. A vast proportion of these suffer from type 2
diabetes, and many suffer for a long time without
having any idea that anything is wrong.

This chronic illness, therefore, often results in secondary
effects like nerve, kidney or cardiovascular damage.
The following list gives some of the most likely symptoms:

- Frequent urination (polyuria) and
nocturnal urination (nocturia)

- Increased thirst (polydipsia)

- Poor appetite and weight loss

- Exhaustion, fatigue and weakness

- Food craving episodes (particularly at
the start of the illness)

- General susceptibility to infection (in particular
infections of the urinary tract and skin)

- Itching

- Headaches, dizziness

- Nausea, vomiting

- Impaired vision

- Muscle cramps

- Cognitive disorders

pancreas can lead to sugar-related illnesses. And so the vicious circle is complete: too much sugar leads to insulin resistance and diminished availability of serotonin. At the same time, low serotonin levels and an agitated state can contribute to insulin resistance, depletion of the insulin reserves and ultimately to type 2 diabetes.

TREATMENTS AND PROGNOSIS

Recognized in the early stages, type 2 diabetes can respond positively to measures to ensure weight loss, a change in eating habits and an increase in physical activity. If these steps alone are not sufficiently successful, then medications can be prescribed. Only when these do not relieve symptoms do you supplement with insulin injections. This by no means suggests that someone who injects themselves once with insulin will always need to inject. As soon as blood sugar values are back in equilibrium, the release of insulin by the body will also function better because the strain on the pancreas is reduced.

Physical Activity

Along with a dietary switch to low-carbohydrate foods, physical exercise is ideal to de-stress the malfunctioning cell metabolism. It doesn't even have to be sporting activity. Just regular walking at a brisk pace and in the fresh air will allow cells to recover and blood pressure as well as blood sugar levels will fall. Oxygen is invigorating and the daylight is mood enhancing.

DENTAL PROBLEMS

Sugar is a real tooth killer. Having said this, it is not just pure sugar in confectionery and honey that contributes to the development of tooth decay, but also in bread, baked goods, cakes or crisps – and even in supposedly healthy foodstuffs such as fruit.

It doesn't matter whether it's glucose, sucrose or fructose: all fermentable carbohydrates can be converted by bacteria. This is easiest of all to achieve with sucrose, closely followed by glucose and fructose. Galactose and lactose are about 20 times less damaging in this respect.

WHAT CAUSES THE DAMAGE?

Sugar doesn't directly damage the teeth. The teeth, however, are covered in a biofilm (plaque), which contains many acid-forming bacteria. These eat the sugar and convert it into acids. The acids dissolve calcium phosphate in the tooth enamel and attack the tooth.

Normally the oral cavity has a neutral pH value between 6 and 7. Sugary foodstuffs push the pH temporarily towards an acidic value between 5 and 4. This means that minerals can break away more easily from the tooth enamel. Because saliva gradually neutralizes the acids, the tooth enamel can recover again. So the development of tooth decay occurs as a result of a cycle of demineralization and remineralization of the dental material.

More important than the type of sugar or the quantity consumed, is the frequency of its consumption, since continuous consumption of sugar lowers the pH value into the acidic range. Eating or drinking regularly throughout the day leads to continuous acid attacks.

Even more dangerous are sweet items that stay longer in the mouth (for example, boiled sweets). Sugars from sweets can accumulate on the teeth and so offer an ideal breeding ground for bacteria. Frequent consumption of soft drinks is particularly damaging. With their high sugar content and acidic pH value they are particularly effective at encouraging demineralization of the tooth enamel.

Effective Treatment

Dental problems such as decay or parodontitis (inflammation of the gums) should always be taken seriously and treated as quickly as possible. A switch to healthy, tooth-friendly sugars is also recommended. Certain monosaccharides such as galactose and xylose, for example, are difficult or impossible for the bacteria to metabolize and so are less likely to cause tooth decay.

The treatment of dental problems is urgent precisely because damaging bacteria can cross over into the neural pathways and the blood stream as soon as they have penetrated or weakened the tooth enamel or gums. In this way they can also pass over into our internal organs. The tooth acts as a point of entry for bacteria which then spread more widely. This bacterial invasion can mean that the immune system is overburdened by chronic irritation and the body can no longer self regulate. In this way, an abscessed tooth root apex can, for example, trigger heart problems. In pregnant women gum disease can increase the risk of premature birth. Decaying teeth can even be a contributory cause of, or trigger for, multiple sclerosis (MS), rheumatism and type 2 diabetes.

What Can You Do?

Brush your teeth daily, morning and evening, with fluoride toothpaste. Ideally you should clean your teeth regularly after every meal. If there is no opportunity to do this you should at least rinse your mouth out with water. Sugar-free or xylitol chewing gum are also suitable occasionally for quick and easy teeth cleaning. They clean the surface area of the teeth and the interdental spaces. Chewing also promotes the production of saliva, which has its own cleaning properties.

HAIR LOSS

Hair is one of the dermal appendages and regenerates itself regularly. Every person loses around 100 hairs per day. This is normal. It only becomes a problem if more hair falls out than grows back again.

The causes of abnormal hair loss are often genetic or hormonal in nature. But stress, environmental toxins, thyroid problems, diabetes, anaemia, crash dieting, a protein deficient diet or contraceptives can lead to greater hair loss. Often the hair loss is delayed and doesn't occur for two or three months. If the relevant cause of the hair loss is removed, then generally the hair will grow back again.

DIETARY INFLUENCES

But poor eating habits contribute more than anything else to hair loss, and particular attention should be paid to the following:

- Saturated fats: in the event of excess quantities of dihydrotestosterone (DHT) the body reacts with increased hair loss. This hormone is produced particularly when too many saturated fats are consumed (like from meat, sausage products and fatty milk products)
- Protein deficiency: in people with a very low protein diet there is a greater danger that physical degeneration processes are strengthened and the ageing process is accelerated. In this context the body slows down or discontinues hair growth.
- Too much salt: high quantities of normal table salt can trigger hair loss. Better options are: sea salt or iodized table salt.
- Sugar: excessive sugar consumption causes a rise in adrenaline levels. As a result of insulin cascades and a rapid drop in insulin, the body goes into stress and releases even greater quantities of the neurotransmitter. Because of the elevated adrenaline levels more androgens (male sex hormones) are released. This in term precipitates premature hair loss.

HORMONAL INFLUENCES

One decisive contributor to hair loss is our stress metabolism. Too much concentrated sugar along with elevated insulin and cortisol levels put a strain on the control of the sex hormone GnRH. Up until the menopause women have relatively high levels of follicle-stimulating hormone (FSH) and oestrogen, and simultaneously lower levels of luteinizing hormone (LH) and progesterone. After the menopause this imbalance often becomes more pronounced: the effects of oestrogen become less powerful, and androgens get the upper hand with consequences for hair. So, for women, hair loss often first occurs during or after the menopause.

The male sex hormone testosterone, an androgen, plays an important role in this so-called androgenic alopecia. The hair follicles react sensitively to androgens and, as a result, the hair grows back less readily, the hair roots shrivel and with time wither away completely.

Dietary Supplements

The change in diet as described on pages 116–19 is recommended, as is a switch to using healthy sugar. Be careful to consume sufficient protein and not too much saturated fat. The trace element zinc also has properties that can be helpful in case of hair loss. In addition, you should include the following substances in your diet or by means of intelligently targeted food supplements: chromium and selenium (see pages 112–13), amino acids and omega-3 fatty acids (see page 104).

SKIN PROBLEMS

Nothing can alter the fact that our skin loses elasticity and develops wrinkles with increasing age. But the speed at which this natural process progresses can certainly be influenced, as suboptimal dietary habits speed up the skin's ageing process.

SIGNS OF AGEING

There is a direct connection between skin ageing and sugar: high concentrations of sugar in the blood lead to a bonding of the collagen fibres in connective tissues.

The sugar reacts with protein and other molecules. As a result, AGEs (Advanced Glycation End products) are produced, which form a bulky mesh in the connective fibres. In this way the skin ultimately loses its elasticity, and wrinkles and tears form in the connective tissues.

So-called glycation is the prime culprit for the development of wrinkles. Furthermore, cell function and the skin's inbuilt repair system are impaired by high sugar consumption.

High sugar or indeed high insulin levels not only accelerate cell ageing, but also set in motion inflammatory cascades within the cells. Inflammatory neurotransmitters from the interleukin and interferon families damage the connective tissues and the skin.

At the same time, inflammatory metabolic by-products from collagen when insulin levels are high can damage the skin and hair. In some circumstances older skin can end up in a state of chronic inflammation. This is apparent in an accelerated ageing of the skin as well as itching and eczema.

CANCER

A sugar-rich diet can play a role in the development of cancer and the growth of cancerous cells insofar as cancer has a very specific metabolism: in order to live, it needs a lot of sugar. Sugar acts to fan the flames, so to speak, for most cancer cells.

High blood sugar levels, such as those that follow the consumption of confectionery, potatoes or white bread, give the cells the ideal fuel. A further driver for any kind of cell growth is insulin. This key hormone also has a strengthening impact on cancer cells, which results in tumour growth being encouraged. In the case of insulin resistance, where blood glucose cannot be exploited by healthy cells, the cancer cells find it even easier to use the blood sugar for their own purposes.

Keeping Blood Sugar Levels in Balance

Reducing levels of insulin can be achieved by consuming less sugar or by using alternatives. A maximum of 40 g (1½ oz) of carbohydrates per meal is recommended by Dr Ulrike Kämmerer of Würzburg University. This encourages the body to switch over to fat burning in order to supply itself with sufficient energy. At the same time, the liver is prompted to produce so-called ketone bodies from fatty acids, which help supply sugar-dependent organs such as the brain with energy in place of the glucose. Within the framework of this kind of ketogenic diet, it is important to ensure sufficient intake of high-quality protein, essential fatty acids and saturated fats, fibre and vital nutrients as well as valuable bioactive plant extracts. At the same time consumption of sugar and starch must be reduced or alternatively substituted by sugar types that barely cause any increase in blood sugar. This will guarantee that the body receives the nutrients it needs so that healthy cells can derive sufficient energy.

The most important aim here is to avoid blood sugar spikes, but to maintain constant blood sugar and insulin levels after meals. Additional physical activity increases the sensitivity of the skeletal muscles to insulin, which makes it easier to keep blood sugar levels in balance and can even reduce insulin resistance.

ADD/ADHD

Around 5 per cent of children and young people between the ages of 3 and 17 are diagnosed with attention deficit disorder or attention deficit hyperactivity disorder (ADD/ADHD) and this is more common among boys than girls. What's more, diagnoses amongst primary school children are increasing.

But this is not a classic childhood illness: around 60 per cent of those affected continue to suffer into adulthood. In ADD/ADHD cases a malfunctioning of the central nervous system occurs, which presents itself in the form of hyper- or hypoactivity (over- or underactivity). An essential role here is played by the neurotransmitter dopamine. Affected children have chronically low dopamine levels. The information exchange between nerve cells is impaired and stimuli cannot be responded to appropriately.

POOR CONCENTRATION

Since babies and children have particularly sensitive nervous systems, they sometimes respond very rapidly and with exaggerated reactions to external stimuli such as noise, visual impressions and certain foodstuffs. Especially after the consumption of confectionery (sugar), many children appear agitated and some also become aggressive and confrontational.

A 2006 study published in the American Journal of Public Health demonstrated that children who consume a lot of soft drinks are often hyperactive or have concentration problems. The discovery was made by a team of research scientists directed by Lars Lien at the University of Oslo. The researchers asked about 5,000 children aged between 15 and 16 about their daily soft drink consumption and also their mental health. In this way the researchers were able to establish a direct link between soft drink consumption and hyperactivity as well as other mental and behavioural disorders.

NEURODEGENERATIVE DISEASES

Any malfunctioning of the sugar metabolism can contribute to a whole range of neurological illnesses. In the brain there is an extensive network of insulin receptors. Insulin is responsible for gene control, growth processes, cell division, programmed cell death and the transmission of insulin signals. It is also involved in the regulation of eating behaviour, smell, the body's tranquillizing system and the pain system and is particularly important for memory and cognitive achievement.

Nowadays it is known that insulin resistance can pave the way for neurodegenerative diseases including Alzheimer's Disease. Insulin resistance in the brain leads to a deterioration in memory performance, memory retention, concentration and cognitive processes. Addictive behaviour, eating disorders, persistent fatigue (chronic fatigue syndrome), depression and dementia are, therefore, as closely linked to insulin resistance as type 2 diabetes. Alongside previous theories about the development of Alzheimer's, this cluster of symptoms is described in more recent publications as type 3 diabetes. Insulin resistance means that brain cells cannot be adequately supplied with glucose. This causes massive damage to the structure and function of the cells and to the component and energy metabolisms.

Diabetes and Dementia

Until recently, the brain was not thought to be one of the organs affected by secondary damage from type 2 diabetes. A current study from the journal *Archives of Neurology* (2012), however, came to the conclusion that a pre-existing diabetes condition was closely associated with accelerated cognitive degeneration in old age. The reason for this is that diabetes results in inflammatory changes in blood vessels throughout the body. The small blood vessels in the brain are particularly seriously affected by this. The result is a reduction in oxygen supply to the brain cells.

Benefits of a Healthy Lifestyle

Many age researchers now think that half of all Alzheimer's cases could be avoided with a healthy lifestyle. Physical activity stimulates the brain, in particular the hippocampus, which is responsible for the process of learning and for memory performance. Regular moderate endurance sport (running, walking, cycling, swimming), strength training and stretching exercises don't just train your body, but also your memory.

The Sunshine Hormone

A balanced Vitamin D level also seems to protect against dementia. Older people are particularly at risk of a shortage of this 'sunshine hormone', since their skin is less responsive to UV light. This is particularly the case in countries with relatively little daylight. In the UK, recent figures indicate that one in five adults and one in six children are at risk of low vitamin D.

An American-British study published in 2009 confirmed that, for participants over the age of 65, those with the lowest vitamin D levels showed double the frequency of comprehension problems than those with high vitamin D values. In animal research too little or too much sleep increased the number of beta amyloid plaques, protein fragments that are found in large quantities in the brains of Alzheimer's sufferers.

The main natural source of vitamin D is through sunlight. Foods containing high vitamin D include oily fish, tofu, eggs and pork and supplements are readily available.

THYROID DISORDERS

Thyroid disorders are often triggered by disturbances in the sugar metabolism; mitochondrial weakness and growing oxidative stress. This metabolic malfunctioning is accompanied by high levels of insulin, inflammatory neurotransmitters, blood sugar, damaging 'sugar-coating' of important signal carriers and energy deficiencies within the inner cell.

To remedy this energy crisis, the thyroid springs into action as an emergency supply system. Activated over long periods of time, the system becomes exhausted and breaks down. The thyroid hormone T_3 (triiodothyronine) rises towards its upper threshold limit, without actually exceeding it, and this hormone is over 100 times more active than the thyroid hormone T_4. T_3 acts as a so-called gene-activating transcription factor, which switches on more than 400 stress adapting genes. These acute emergency systems handle short-term stress situations. Deployed long term, they cause illness, facilitate inflammation and obstruct natural repair processes.

ANTIOXIDANT PROTECTION

Scientific studies also show that high dosages of certain antioxidants are well suited to strengthen the cell protection system against radical damage and to support the body's own defence mechanisms. The most important antioxidant substances include vitamins B, C and E, flavonoids, extracts from grape skin and colourful vegetables, selenium, alpha lipoic acids, N-acetyl cysteine, nicotinamide, bioflavonoids and omega-3 fatty acids (fish oils). High-dose combinations of these natural substances can work synergistically to reduce the inflammation process and the disordered immune system can be put back on the right track. Various drugs are available to treat these conditions but both selenium and zinc have been shown to be helpful too.

CHRONIC PAIN

In the USA, 116 million people suffer from chronic pain, in the UK this figure is 7 to 8 million people. These symptoms are triggered and subsequently underpinned by pathologically elevated blood sugar values, insulin resistance and sugar utilization disorders.

HOW PAIN MANIFESTS

The malfunctioning metabolic system puts a strain on muscle and liver fat cells and swamps the body with free fatty acids. Free fatty acids, hyperglycaemia and hyperinsulinaemia lead directly to inflammations as does the inflammatory substance cytokine (actually a fundamental part of the immune defence system). The consequences include fibromyalgia (muscle fibre pain), migrant pain syndrome and irritated connective tissue, blood vessel changes, fatty liver disease, bottlenecks in the muscle energy metabolism and inflammatory irritation of the central nervous system.

The insulin resistance creates energy deficiencies. Without sufficient energy, there is an increase in the metabolic waste products lactate and ammonia. The muscles hurt and their performance is compromised. Because there is a relative shortage of oxygen, an increased number of free radicals are produced, which further impede the functioning of the mitochondria and their key enzymes.

In many patients these energy deficiencies along with muscle pain and muscle weakness result in reduced physical activity. This relative inertia with minimal sugar combustion, leads in the longer term to heart attack, stroke and type 2 diabetes.

PAIN-FREE, SUGAR-FREE

Tense and painful muscles are also a consequence of the damaging influence of ammonia (NH_1) on the brain. This by-product of metabolic decomposition attacks the chloride tubules in the muscles, causing tension, which doctors seek to alleviate by prescribing medications such as Musaril, Temesta, Tavor or Valium. Instead of taking medication on which you can become psychologically or physically dependent, it would be better to avoid the production of

ammonia by switching to a sugar free diet. The more carbohydrates and sugar you consume, the more the body generates ammonia. The less sugar consumed (and thus the more economic the energy metabolism), the lower the amounts of ammonia produced. The chloride tubules in the muscles stay relaxed and no pain develops.

DIETARY CHANGES

The scientific data on this is clear. A huge number of excellent studies show that it is possible to reduce considerably the strain on your body, to lessen any susceptibility to inflammation and to alleviate pain by implementing the following dietary changes: reduce the consumption of 'bad', simple carbohydrates (for example in bread, pizza, sugar, potatoes, confectionery) and, instead, favour healthy complex carbohydrates (in vegetables and pulses); consume valuable proteins and fats (in meat, fish, eggs, goat and sheep's cheese, vegetable oils, nuts and seeds) and ensure an intake of fibre and other vital substances in low-glucose and low-fructose fruits like berries, papaya, grapefruit, pineapple, apricots and peaches. Above all, avoid consumption of carbohydrates in the evening to reap far-reaching health rewards.

If appropriate, taking antioxidant protective substances like vitamin E, vitamin C, vitamin B or alpha-lipoic acid can be an effective way of supporting dietary change. If metabolic equilibrium can be restored via one of these methods, this then creates an opportunity to undertake complementary treatments such as physiotherapy, osteopathy, or manual, neuromyological or myoreflex therapy.

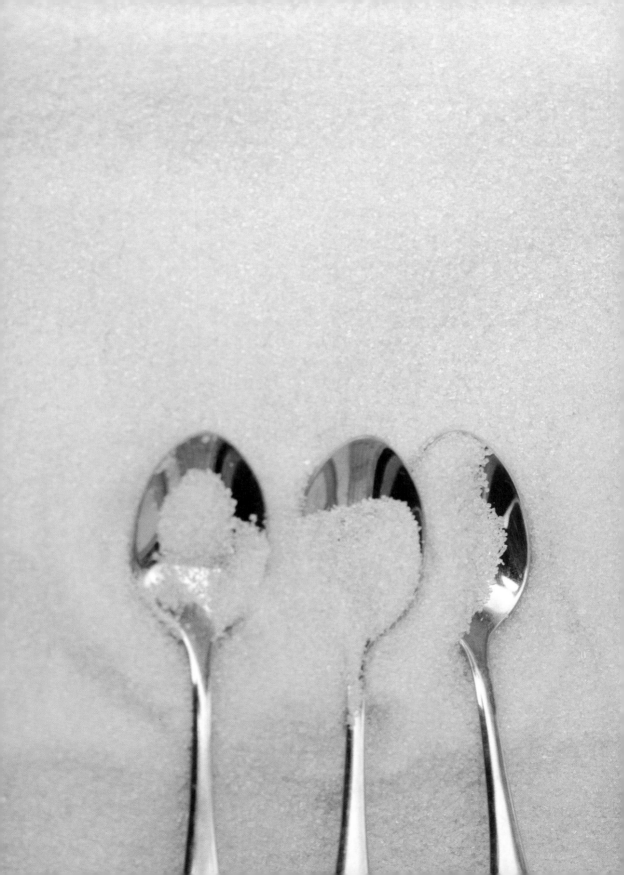

4

The 3-Step
Sugar Detox Plan

*Follow this 3-step withdrawal
programme and kick your sugar habit for
good. First assess the foods that you are
eating right now, learn how to replace
them with healthier alternatives and
then follow the simple and effective
12-week diet and exercise programme.*

ONE STEP AT A TIME

It can take as long as 12 weeks to wean your body off sugar and reset your natural rhythms. This three-step, sugar detox plan looks to help you discover your own sugar traps, find healthier alternatives and get in the habit of regular exercise to use up your sugar stocks.

Step 1: Preparation

Before embarking on any new food regime, you have to examine your current eating habits. This section encourages you to keep a log of the foods you eat over a given period – say, one week – so that you can properly assess which of your habits need changing.

Step 2: Know Your Foods

The success of the cure is wholly dependent on maintaining a healthy, balanced diet. This section outlines the main food groups available to you and offers advice on how and when best to incorporate them into your new food regime.

Step 3: Diet and Exercise

At the core of the cure is a sensible eating and exercise plan – a 12-week programme that allows your to redress your eating habits and get active. First you'll establish a food regime that determines when to eat certain foods and in what quantities. Then you will work out an exercise routine that fits in with your eating habits and lifestyle.

Step 1
Preparation

The first step of the cure is to analyse your current diet. What are you eating right now and which of those foods are high in sugar content? Think also about when you are eating, and whether simple changes to your daily routine can help eliminate sugar-loaded snacks.

WHAT DO YOU EAT?

As we have seen, sugar is everywhere in the diet: it is in bread, it is in pizza and it is nearly always in any food that is in a packet. If you are going to beat this addiction, then the first step is to identify just where this sugar is coming from. The scientific way to do this is to keep a food diary. Write down everything you eat each day – after eating each meal, if possible. Be honest with yourself: you need to diagnose exactly where your lifestyle lets the sugar in.

In a stressful, busy environment it is easy enough to overlook the odd chocolate bar, the odd fizzy drink, and lack of exercise because we are stuck in the car or in meetings all day. Use the diary to find out where you stand and what foods you could banish from the fridge and pantry. Don't make things any more difficult by leaving temptations around the house or at work.

An inventory cannot cure you on its own but it can let you know what you are dealing with. This is how we might do it as doctors – you may not want to be quite as medical about it, but it helps to see how a thorough approach works.

KEEPING A DIARY

Keep a log of the food you are eating on a daily basis.
In the hustle and bustle of everyday life valuable insights are all
too quickly lost. Your records will help you to stay permanently
on the ball. Here are some tips on how to go about it.

1. Spare No Detail

Meticulously note down when you eat and what you eat,
including ingredients, nutrients, spices and so on. And, of course, what you
drink. Check the labelling on any packets and make a note. If you are eating
out in canteens or restaurants, it can be more difficult to keep an accurate
record, so you may need to do a bit of detective work.

2. Look For Patterns

Make notes about when you feel hunger. How long are the gaps between
eating something and thinking about eating something else? See if you
can establish connections between different moods – stress, conflict,
boredom – at the times when you feel hungry.

3. Monitor Your Moods

Try to feel conscious of how certain foods (especially new, unfamiliar things
you might like to try) affect your mental and physical condition.

4. How Are You Sleeping?

Make a note of your sleep patterns and see if they may change depending
on what you ate the evening before. How hungry are you at breakfast time?

5. Record Bursts of Activity

Note down the times at which you are physically active every day,
and for how long. This should include basic activities like walking to the
shops, up the stairs and carrying shopping as well as visits to the gym or a
long walk. All movement impacts on blood sugar levels.

YOUR FOOD LOG

A food log helps to slowly but surely guide you to what you want to eat and how to avoid any pitfalls. All you need is a notebook, preferably with calendar and schedules. Give yourself a few days, perhaps even a week to diagnose what is going on with your diet. You have got the rest of your life to give up sugar so there is no rush. Self-observation is important.

SETTING REASONABLE GOALS

Starting tomorrow, you should aim to make healthy and wholesome food for all of your meals. It sounds simple and yet the day-to-day implementation of such an aim often proves far more difficult. It is one thing writing a plan, quite another implementing it. This is especially true if you enjoy your food. Have faith – a sugar-free diet can still taste good and be something to look forward to each day. It is a mindful approach.

Staying on Track

Don't be too hard on yourself or your family. Try to get them involved and excited too, but remember to be patient and keep things within reason. Set yourself achievable goals – even cutting down the sugar you are currently eating by half is a good start. And if you have children, encourage them to join you on the journey. If everyone is on board, it's a lot easier to stick to your good intentions.

Ideally, you should start on a weekend, go shopping together and then gather in the kitchen. Cooking and eating should always be done in a relaxed atmosphere that is fun and motivated. You may be cooking new things, but these will soon become favourites. Behavioural psychologists have found that the best way to alter lifelong cultural, regional or family food habits is to make the experience joyful and introduce change through a passion for good food.

ELIMINATING SUGAR TRAPS

First things first: clear out the fridge and pantry. Get rid of everything sweet or with hidden sugars in it. When you go shopping, concentrate on buying the best-quality foods – so you know that what you are going to eat in the future is the best and worth your time and effort.

Sugar-Free Recipes

If you need guidance when it comes to preparing balanced, sugar-free meals, turn to the recipe section (pages 132–71). They have been developed by chef Thorsten Probost and culinary consultant Drew Smith, and can get you started straight away with these high-quality, balanced, sugar-free meals. In addition to these, it pays to bear in mind the following:

- Buy organic: treat yourself to lean cuts like beef fillet – you are not giving all your money to the sugar industry now, so you can afford to spend it on yourself and your loved ones.
- Vary your protein: your intake of protein can come from a variety of sources including fresh fish, eggs, yoghurt and soya.
- Buy plenty of vegetables: they are often inexpensive and are worth getting to know.
- Take care with dairy: these products are allowed, but always check the label first.
- Change your carbohydrates: switch to wholegrain carbohydrates for pasta, rice and flour.

Step 2
Know Your Foods

It is not enough simply to eliminate sugary foods from your diet. You need also to find out how best to replace them. Get to know the major food groups and the roles they should play in your new food regime.

WHAT IS A HEALTHY DIET?

A healthy diet – one that supplies any organism with the most important nutrients – provides the ideal conditions for greater physical performance and good health. Even our mental well-being is affected by dietary habits, and this has an important impact on hormonal activity. What you eat, therefore, affects every aspect of your life: how you feel, how you look, how fit and creative you are, how you sleep and how fast you age. Bad eating habits often arise because people simply know too little about healthy eating or have never really learned how to eat properly.

A common problem is an excessive consumption of carbohydrates and fat along with an insufficient intake of protein, vitamins and minerals. Considering the complex metabolic processes in our bodies, people actually need a very manageable quantity of nutrients, but these must always remain in correct proportion to each other. In addition, the body needs a regular supply of certain substances like essential fatty acids, amino acids, vitamins, minerals and trace elements, preferably supplied in accordance with our regular daily rhythms. Only these can ensure that the body's substances are replenished and regenerated.

Dietary Building Blocks

Eating healthily is essentially very simple. You just need to understand what's important if you are going to be confident when tackling the sometimes confusing range of options in the supermarket or on a restaurant menu. If you can do this, you'll find out what is best for you. Focus on fresh, top-quality and unprocessed foodstuffs. They taste better and supply you with valuable nutrients. Eating in this way will have a significant impact on your quality of life.

A MEDITERRANEAN DIET

Today it is generally agreed that the body is best supplied with all necessary nutrients by consuming a varied, balanced, mixed diet modelled on Mediterranean eating habits. A diet of this kind supports the immune system and the body's self-regulatory functions.

Traditional Mediterranean fare doesn't follow any particular nutritional programme. And its healthy properties aren't so much connected with individual foodstuffs as with the interplay of the ingredients. There is abundant consumption of seasonal fruit and vegetables, cereal products like (wholemeal) bread, noodles (pasta) and rice, potatoes, pulses, nuts and seeds, fresh or dried herbs and garlic, saltwater fish, 'white' meat such as poultry and natural olive oil. Milk and dairy products and eggs are consumed in moderation. And beef, pork and lamb as well as sausages are traditionally found only occasionally on the menu.

Health Benefits

This combination of foods results in the optimum balance of nutrients with few saturated (animal) fatty acids and an abundance of monounsaturated and polyunsaturated fatty acids (in particular omega-3 fatty acids). Equally positive is the high content of organic high quality protein, 'good' carbohydrates, dietary fibre, minerals, trace elements as well as vitamins and antioxidants.

Research has demonstrated that this combination improves the composition of blood fats by lowering the levels of damaging LDL cholesterol and triglycerides and in return increasing levels of 'healthy' HDL cholesterol. This kind of diet reduces the oxidation of fats, lowers the risk of blood vessel clotting and counteracts any inflammatory processes. In this way the Mediterranean diet guarantees a (relatively) long life, even if you are already suffering from a chronic illness. This was the conclusion of an Italian group of doctors working under research director Francesco Sofi on the meta analysis of twelve large international studies, which recorded the eating habits of a total of 1.5 million people over a time period of between 3 and 18 years.

PROTEIN

Proteins are essential for a thriving human body. They are primary building blocks in the make up of body tissue, and can also be an important fuel source. Protein constitutes the source of all life and, along with fats and carbohydrates, belongs to the major nutrients. It delivers as much energy as carbohydrate (4.1 kcal/g).

Certain protein building blocks are important elements in the cell walls (membranes) and are responsible for the exchange of substances there. Others are responsible for the essential transport of oxygen in the blood. Other proteins regulate biochemical processes in our bodies by means of different enzymes and hormones, and take care of physical and mental capabilities and our emotional well-being. Without the proteins in our muscles we would not be able to move.

Proteins always consist of individual components called amino acids. The number of components and the sequence in which they are linked determine the characteristics of the protein. There are a total of 20 amino acids and a proportion of these (for adults it is 8, for children as many as 10) are particularly important (vital even), because the body cannot generate them itself.

Sugar from Protein

In periods of extended stress and when your body's ready sugar stores are empty (for example as a result of a diet low in carbohydrates), proteins can also contribute to the process of energy production. The amino acids that result from the breakdown of protein can be used by the body to produce its own glucose in a process is known as gluconeogenesis.

These protein building blocks must, therefore, be obtained from food. If our diet contains too few of these essential amino acids, deficiency symptoms can occur. The essential amino acids for adults are: isoleucine, leucine, lysine, methionine, phenylalanine, threonine, tryptophan, valine.

FEELING FULL

Protein is particularly good for making you feel full for longer and so can help prevent food cravings and maintain blood sugar at a constant level. Nowadays it is also suggested that a balanced intake of protein from lean meat, fish, pulses, yoghurt and cheese can have a beneficial influence on fat metabolism and fat distribution.

However, the body can only store small quantities of protein. So an adult needs to consume at least 55–85 g (2–3 oz) of protein per day. Even so, just two or three meals per week containing small quantities of meat or fish can suffice, with vegetarian dishes covering the remaining requirements as protein is also found in plants (cereals, pulses, soya).

Animal proteins (meat, fish, eggs, milk, dairy products) are particularly valuable because they contain all the essential amino acids the body requires (see opposite).

Vegetable proteins can be used just as effectively as long as they are varied (for example muesli with milk, jacket potatoes with quark, lentil soup with wholemeal bread) and eaten throughout the day.

HEALTHY GRAINS

Bread is widely eaten throughout the Western world. Many nations have a rich variety of breads, most of which are produced from wheat, which is rich in starch and so causes blood sugar and insulin levels to shoot up rapidly after consumption. In addition, wheat contains a lot of gluten, a protein that, if consumed frequently, can cause chronic damage to the small intestine. Fortunately the small intestine can almost always recover by consuming gluten-free foods. If dietary habits can be changed before it's too late, the intestinal mucosa can be partially or even completely regenerated.

Healthy alternatives include gluten-free grains and grasses such as buckwheat, amaranth, kaniwa, millet, barley, quinoa or ancient grain varieties. Other ancient grains such as einkorn, wild emmer and spelt do contain relatively little gluten or more easily tolerated proteins, but they are not suitable for people with coeliac disease. If, however, you are 'just' trying to reduce the sugar in your diet and still want to enjoy breads and pastries, then these grain types are ideal. They are rich in valuable amino acids and contain significantly more secondary plant substances and minerals.

FATS

Even though fats deliver more than twice as much energy as carbohydrates and proteins, they don't necessarily make you fat when you eat them. In fact they play a crucial role in regulating blood sugar levels and, therefore, in the feeling of fullness after a meal. If carbohydrates are combined with fats or oils (for example wholemeal pasta with a salmon and cream sauce or white bread with olive oil) glucose levels in the blood rise more slowly. Ultimately the body also has to digest the fat. A similar effect is evident when carbohydrates are combined with protein.

In addition, certain fats are crucial for the body since, like protein, they act as essential building materials; for example for cell walls (membranes) and for various hormones. Last but not least, fats are carriers of secondary plant products or phytochemicals, as well as fat soluble vitamins E, D, A and K which the body otherwise cannot utilize. When necessary the body can also convert glycerine, a component of natural fats and oils, into glucose.

Bear in mind, however, that any surplus of nutritional fat can be stored by the body in almost limitless amounts in fatty deposits on the stomach, legs and bottom – with inevitable consequences for your figure and, ultimately, your health.

GOOD FATS, BAD FATS

The quality of a particular fat is determined by its chemical composition. All nutritional fats consist of glycerine and fatty acids, whereby the fatty acids form long carbon chains. Three types of fatty acids can be distinguished:

- saturated fatty acids, in which the carbon atoms are connected to one another by single bonds
- monounsaturated fatty acids, which have a double bonded carbon atom in addition to the single bonded carbons
- polyunsaturated fatty acids with multiple double bonds

Saturated Fatty Acids

These are found in large quantities in animal foodstuffs such as meat, eggs, cheese, cold meats as well as animal fats such as butter and lard. Because of their single bonded carbons they react more slowly with other chemical substances in the body and so, apart from energy production, they are not useful for any other important, beneficial or regulative processes. In excess (more than 20 g/1 oz per day) they can even cause damage to the body.

Unsaturated Fatty Acids

These can have significant health benefits and are even essential to some extent. Vegetable oils like rapeseed, soya, flax, walnut or safflower are rich in monounsaturated fatty acids.

Polyunsaturated Fatty Acids

These are divided into omega-3 and omega-6 fatty acids. They are important components of the cell membranes. The flexible long-chained fatty acids help keep the cell's outer membrane flexible and they are the base material for so-called eicosanoids ('tissue hormones') which are involved in a vast number of metabolic processes. For instance, they regulate blood pressure, lower cholesterol levels and curb inflammatory processes.

Omega-3 fatty acids considerably reduce the risk of cardio-vascular disease. They also have a positive impact on our visual function. It is possible they may help to prevent so-called macular degeneration, which can lead to blindness. Furthermore, it appears that high omega-3 fatty acid levels could have a positive impact on depressive illnesses and other emotional disorders. Because of their anti-inflammatory properties, they can help alleviate pain and reduce bone or tissue degeneration in patients suffering from rheumatism.

CARBOHYDRATES

Carbohydrates were long considered by scientists primarily as a pure supplier of energy. Carbohydrates can supply as much energy as protein (4.1 kcal/g) and they ensure that we feel full quickly. If a meal is rich in sugar, the body even has a preference to utilize this first because the energy from sugar is available to the metabolic system more quickly and with less processing effort. But despite this, the body can survive perfectly well without carbohydrates. They do not belong to the group of essential nutrients.

There is, therefore, no real physiological reason to consume carbohydrates regularly. Furthermore, excessive consumption of simple carbohydrates in desserts, bread, fruit juices, fizzy drinks etc. along with a simultaneous deficit in healthy fats and essential vitamins leads to a derailing of the healthy and balanced relationships in our body. Toxic metabolic by-products, environmental toxins and free radicals from oxidative stress can accumulate and pave the way for poor health and eventually serious illness. So as part of the dietary changes designed to overcome or avoid sugar addiction it is necessary to avoid these quick carbohydrates.

Complex Carbohydrates

'Good' (complex) carbohydrates, on the other hand, guarantee a gradual increase in blood sugar levels (and subsequently a correspondingly slower fall in blood sugar levels). As well as containing energy, complex carbohydrates provide essential vitamins and minerals as well as filling dietary fibre which is beneficial for our digestion. In this way they help maintain blood sugar at a constant level for longer. The result is that you feel full for longer and experience far fewer food cravings.

HEALTHY SUGARS

Sugar plays a crucial role in many bodily functions, so it is useful to know which sugars can be considered healthy.

D-galactose

Galactose is a monosaccharide and primarily found in milk and dairy products, but also in chickpeas, berries and lentils. The galactose powder that can be bought through various internet suppliers or larger pharmacies is a distillate of milk and milk sugar (lactose). In cooking, galactose powder can be used in hot and cold dishes and for baking.

Xylose

Xylose is a monosaccharide found in some varieties of berries, but mostly in bark and other parts of certain trees and plants. Xylose is often sold as 'xylitol' powder, a hydrogenated form of xylose, which is widely available in stores and online. It has 90 per cent of the sweetness of household sugar.

Erythritol

This sweet-tasting powder is extracted from grape sugar (glucose) or household sugar (sucrose). It can be used in different foodstuffs from confectionery to dairy products. It can also be used as a sweetener.

Trehalose

Trehalose consists of two glucose molecules bonded together and occurs naturally in various plants and fungi such as sunflower seeds and shiitake mushrooms. Trehalose powder has a gentle sweetness, is kind to teeth and protects the body's natural protein structures. In addition, insulin levels only rise very slightly after consumption. It has about half the sweetness of household sugar. You can use trehalose among other things to sweeten beverages, baked goods and ice cream.

Isomaltulose

Isomaltulose (sometimes packaged as Palatinose) occurs in small quantities in honey and sugar cane. Blood sugar levels rise more slowly after consumption than they do with 'normal' sugar, because this is a disaccharide rather than a monosaccharide and it must first be broken down in the intestine. Isomaltulose powder has around 70 per cent of the sweetness of household sugar and is well suited to baking.

Ribose

Naturally occurring in the body, ribose improves cardiac output, brain metabolism, the energy metabolism of our muscles, mitochondrial function and the regeneration metabolism. This monosaccharide does not cause a rise in blood sugar levels and acts as a powerful antioxidant. Ribose has around a quarter of the sweetness of household sugar and in addition tastes slightly bitter. It is well suited as a sugar substitute in desserts and drinks, also because it is readily soluble.

Stevia

Stevia is a plant mainly cultivated in Japan, Malaysia, Korea, China, Thailand, Israel and Mexico. It is also licensed in New Zealand and the USA. In 2011 the European Food Safety Authority (EFSA) declared that stevia is neither carcinogenic nor damaging to our genes nor associated with fertility disorders. This ruling allowed the sweetener to be used in yoghurts, muesli, drinks, chocolate and other confectionery within Europe. For home cooking, stevia can be used as a powder, as leaves or as a liquid extract for cold and warm dishes and for baking.

All these sugars or sweeteners are easily available to buy over the internet, or they can be bought or ordered at larger health-food retail chains. Readers keen to introduce these or other sugar supplements into their diets should always consult a health-care professional before doing so.

VITAMINS, MINERALS AND TRACE ELEMENTS

Vitamins don't deliver any energy themselves, but they do ensure the operation of various metabolic, growth, renewal, repair and healing processes. Meanwhile, the proportion of a person's body weight made up by minerals and trace elements amounts to a miniscule 0.01 per cent. Like vitamins, they do not themselves supply any energy.

OBTAINING VITAMINS

Because our bodies cannot produce vitamins themselves, or at least not in sufficient quantities, they must be obtained from our diet. In theory everyone should be able to meet their vitamin requirements from a varied diet. But despite such an overwhelming offering of foodstuffs, vitamin deficiencies are not uncommon. The causes are too little variety, too few fresh foods and too much stress. Also smoking, excessive alcohol consumption, chronic illness, medication or diseases of the digestive system can all drain the body's scarce vitamin reserves.

A sugar-rich diet almost always goes hand in hand with insufficient variety and poor-quality food. So, in order specifically to build up vitamin stores again, foods low in sugar are recommended such as vegetables, raw foods and salad.

Vitamins are distinguished according to whether they dissolve in water or fat. Water-soluble vitamins (with the exception of vitamin B12) can only be stored for a short time, if at all. Fat-soluble vitamins can be stored in the body and can only be absorbed by the body in combination with fat. For this reason you should use a little vegetable oil or butter when you are preparing carrots (vitamin A) or broccoli (vitamin K). See pages 110–11 for a table of important vitamins.

MINERAL PROPERTIES

Minerals assist the digestion of our food, ensure a healthy complexion, strengthen our brain function and therefore our mental agility, are involved in the construction of bones and teeth and regulate blood pressure, nerve and muscle function as well as various enzymes. Trace elements make a significant contribution to hormonal and enzymatic reactions and are present in many proteins.

In recent decades changes in agricultural growing conditions have caused a steady fall in the quantities of minerals and trace elements in our food. As a result of this, ever-increasing numbers of people are showing signs of corresponding deficiencies. The body cannot produce micronutrients itself and it also loses them through sweat, urine and blood.

An unbalanced diet with high quantities of animal proteins often accompanies high levels of sugar consumption and can lead to mineral deficiencies as well as profuse sweating or diarrhoea. A temporary deficiency can be compensated for by the body by excreting fewer minerals and trace elements and absorbing more from the intestine. But if there is a long-term shortfall in supplies then the immune system is weakened and this leads to illness.

You should therefore try to ensure that your body is supplied with sufficient micronutrients. See pages 112–13 for a table of important minerals.

IMPORTANT VITAMINS

FAT-SOLUBLE VITAMINS

RDI = Recommended daily intake

NAME	FUNCTION	SOURCES	RDI
Vitamin A (retinol)	Important for our vision, for reproduction as well as for generating and maintaining skin and mucosal tissues.	Good sources are liver, cod liver oil, saltwater fish, egg yolks, butter, cheese and milk.	1–1.5 mg
Vitamin D (calciferol)	Important for bone structure, teeth, the nervous system and immune system; it promotes absorption of calcium, has an important role in hormone metabolism and has cancer inhibiting properties.	Vitamin D is formed in the skin if there is sufficient sunlight. During periods of the year when there is little natural light it must be artificially supplied.	15–40 µg*
Vitamin E	Blocker of free radicals, important for our immune defence system and cell protection. There are eight different forms of vitamin E. It is particularly important here to distinguish between tocopherols and tocotrienols.	Gamma-tocotrienol is only available from natural sources (vegetable oils, black salsify and nuts). It is accordingly rarer, and yet has a more significant impact on our health. It acts as a powerful antioxidant, slows down the ageing process and prolongs life, reduces inflammation, has a positive effect on blood fat values and has cancer preventing properties.	15–25 mg
Vitamin K	Important for blood clotting and for bones.	Good sources are green vegetables, salad leaves and cabbage.	50–100 µg

* µg = microgram

WATER-SOLUBLE VITAMINS

RDI = Recommended daily intake

NAME	FUNCTION	SOURCES	RDI
Vitamin B1 (thiamine)	Important for energy metabolism and the nervous system. Individual requirements rise with increased energy consumption and in the case of chronic alcohol misuse.	Pork, liver, wholemeal and cereal products and pulses.	1–20 mg
Vitamin B2	Important for metabolic processes.	Milk and dairy products, meat, fish, eggs and mushrooms.	1–20 mg
Vitamin B3 (niacin)	Important in the synthesis and breakdown of carbohydrates, fat and amino acids.	Meat, giblets, fish, eggs and milk.	1–25 mg
Vitamin B6 (pyridoxine)	Important in all enzymatic processes, in haematopoiesis (the formation of blood cells) as well as being crucial for the immune and nervous systems.	Good sources are poultry, pork, fish, pulses, potatoes, avocado, bananas, wholemeal grains and wholegrain products.	1–20 mg
Folic acid	Important for growth, cell regeneration and cell division as well as haematopoiesis.	Strawberries, leafy vegetables, salad, cabbage, asparagus, grains and pulses.	200–400 µg
Biotin	Important for breaking down amino acids and for the biosynthesis of fatty acids.	Liver, egg yolk, nuts, oats, sardines, cauliflower and mushrooms.	20–50 µg
Vitamin B12 (cobalamin)	Significant for folic acid function and haematopoiesis.	Liver, meat, fish, eggs, cheese and milk, but also sauerkraut.	1–5 µg
Vitamin C	Essential for blocking free radicals, as a reducing agent, for the processing of plant-based iron and for the immune system.	Fruits such as kiwi, oranges or sea buckthorn as well as vegetables such as peppers, potatoes, brassicas, salad and herbs.	100–500 mg

IMPORTANT MINERALS

RDI = Recommended daily intake

NAME	FUNCTION	SOURCES	RDI
Chloride	a component of stomach acid, it contributes to maintaining the acid-base balance.	Usually you get enough from table salt, salty foods and mineral water.	600–800 mg
Chromium	as a building block for vitamin B12 this is important for haematopoiesis.	It is contained in almost all foodstuffs and in particularly high proportions in animal products.	80–150 µg
Iron	important for oxygen transport in the blood, for the synthesis of red blood and muscle pigment substances as well as defending against radicals.	Good sources are meat, liver, salmon, oats, wheat germ, pulses, chard and spinach.	10–30 mg
Fluoride	good for the stability of bones and teeth, guards against dental decay.	Good sources are black tea, mineral and tap water, saltwater fish, wholemeal bread and spinach.	1–3.8 mg
Iodine	important for thyroid activity.	Good sources are saltwater fish, milk, iodized table salt as well as foods produced with added iodized salt such as cold meats and cheeses.	100–230 µg
Potassium	significant for the distribution of water around the body and for all excretion processes as well as muscle and heart activity.	Good sources are fish, meat, vegetables, fruit (particularly melons, berries) and cereal products.	1000–1250 mg
Calcium	important for the stability of bones and teeth, for blood clotting as well as for nerve and muscle function.	Good sources are milk and dairy products, broccoli, kale, spinach and leeks.	500–1000 mg
Copper	supports iron in the process of haematopoiesis, an integral part of pigments.	Good sources are fruit, vegetables, nuts and wholemeal products.	1–1.5 mg

NAME	FUNCTION	SOURCES	RDI
Magnesium	important for transmission of stimuli and for muscle contraction.	Good sources are cereal products, pulses, fruit, vegetables and lean pork.	200–400 mg
Manganese	a fundamental component of important enzymes, it contributes to the construction of bone and cartilage.	Good sources are bread, grains, pulses, nuts, spinach, blueberries and black tea.	2–5 mg
Molybdenum	a fundamental component of enzymes, protects against tooth decay.	Contained in almost all foodstuffs.	50–150 µg
Sodium	important for hydration management, muscles, nerves and regulating blood pressure.	Good sources are table salt, salty foods and mineral water.	500 mg
Nickel	activates insulin as well as other hormones and enzymes.	Good sources are grains, pulses and nuts.	0.2–0.5 mg
Phosphorous	important for bone formation, energy transmission and the generation of cell membranes.	Phosphorous is contained in almost all foodstuffs.	700–1250 mg
Selenium	important for defending against damaging radicals.	Good sources are eggs, fish, meat, giblets, porcini mushrooms, nuts, pulses and wholemeal products.	30–100 µg
Silicon	preserves the elasticity of the connective tissues.	Good sources are potatoes, oats and wholemeal products.	5–20 mg
Zinc	an integral component of many enzymes, important for tissue repair and for the immune system.	Good sources are meat, cheese and wholemeal products.	5–15 mg

Step 3
Diet and Exercise

A new food regime with the right food groups will ensure that you are eating the best foods, in the right quantities at the optimum time of day. Combine this meal plan with regular exercise over a period of 12 weeks, and you'll be well on your way to kicking your sugar habit.

THE MEAL PLAN ...

By now your food log will have revealed how much sugar you are eating and what your particular sugar-weaknesses are. You have also learned, however, how to provide your body with all the essential nutrients it really needs. Now you are ready and prepared to finally rid yourself of bad sugar habits by following the diet and exercise plan.

Our plan is suitable for people of any age and has been successfully employed for many years as a complementary therapy for various complaints. Furthermore, unlike other withdrawal programmes, there is no need to give up on sweet things completely. Using healthy sugars in your cooking is allowed, since it can be helpful in stressful situations that might trigger cravings for sweetness.

Our plan is an easy and effective way to harmonize your blood sugar and insulin levels, balancing your metabolism, curing diet-related illnesses and strengthening the immune system. Essentially it comes down to retraining your eating habits: valuable fats, healthy sugars, long-chain carbohydrates, protein-rich foods and healthy fruits all help to restore a malfunctioning sugar metabolism.

This approach also makes the most of unprocessed foods, that are rich in natural vitamins and minerals, which are valuable metabolic aids. Magnesium, zinc, chromium and iron play a role in more than 300 important metabolic processes in the muscles, the nervous system, the brain, the immune system and all internal organs.

Meanwhile, vitamins C and E, protect against cell stress and free radicals, and along with the B vitamin family, they also boost your metabolism as well as supporting cell regeneration.

... AND HOW IT WORKS

For the best results the plan should be followed for a period of at least 12 weeks. Over this time-frame you will be able to retrain your body and bid a confident farewell to sugar by effectively re-balancing your sugar metabolism in combination with a gentle exercise programme.

During the first four weeks you should drastically reduce your consumption of all 'bad' carbohydrates (see page 24 and meal planning overleaf). 'Good', slow-metabolizing carbohydrates, such wholemeal grains and pulses are allowed, but only up until 2 pm for the first eight weeks of the plan. The body needs the hours after this as a break from sugar and insulin.

Only in this way does the body have sufficient time for cell regeneration and repair. From the ninth week onwards, however, this time limit rises to 6 pm.

And the good news is that, apart from unhealthy sugars and flours (as well as processed foods made using them), you hardly need to give up any other foods at all.

REGULAR MEALTIMES

Our plan for a sugar-free life doesn't require you to pay strict attention to your daily calorie intake. It is far more important to supply your body with the right nutrients at the right times.

During the first four weeks it is essential to establish a pattern of three regular meal each day. Sticking to the breaks between meals will help you to develop a healthy feeling of hunger again and encourage fat burning to occur as efficiently as possible.

And if you find the breaks between meals difficult to start with, small snacks that won't put a burden on insulin levels are also suggested on page 119 and recipes on pages 152–5.

DAILY MEAL PLANNING

The success of the plan relies on regular meals that keep your body feeling fulfilled, so that symptoms of sugar withdrawal are quelled. Straying from the advice below will hinder your progress, but it is important to remember that if you do slip up or submit to a craving that all is not lost, get back on the plan and stick to it as quickly as you can. You can always add an extra day to the end of the programme rather than abandoning all your hard work at the first hurdle. The notes below should help you stick to the cure and ensure your cravings are well managed.

BREAKFASTS

In the morning our bodies need an extra dose of energy, making this the right time for carbohydrates, since these are the fastest suppliers of energy. It is important that you choose the right kind of carbohydrates.

- muesli (see recipe, page 140)
- wholemeal bread or bread rolls
- poultry or other lean cold meat (such as roast beef), goat's cheese or sheep's milk cheese
- eggs prepared in a variety of ways (for example soft boiled, in an omelette, scrambled or as pancakes)
- fresh fruit such as apples, pears, bananas, grapes and oranges (although limit your intake, try to combine them with either protein or fat to slow down the release of carbohydrates into the blood stream and note that fruit should be avoided later on in the day, since they contain high levels of glucose and fructose)
- lactose-free cows' milk and cows' milk products such as cheese, natural yoghurt or quark; an alternative option is sheep or goat's milk products

---

LUNCHES

Until 2 pm, you can still eat 'slow-release' carbohydrates (for example in the form of wholemeal grains or pulses). Combine these with meat, fish or soya products as well as generous helpings of vegetables and salad.

- meat (poultry, beef or venison)
- fish (halibut, herring, cod, mackerel, sardines, haddock, plaice, swordfish, sole, tuna, wild salmon but also freshwater fish such as river trout or perch

SUPPERS

For at least the first eight weeks your evening meals should not contain any carbohydrates at all. Only once you reach the ninth week are carbohydrates permitted up until 6 pm. As long as you eat very early, wholegrain bread and pasta are not a problem.

- meat (poultry, beef or venison)
- fish
- vegetables and salad
- poultry or other lean meats (such as beef or chicken breast)
- sheep or goat's cheese
- eggs prepared in a variety of ways (no pancakes or other recipes in which flour is used)

SNACKS

It is important to try to stick to your pattern of three main meals each day, but if you are finding it very difficult then these are the snacks to turn to.

- 1 hard-boiled egg
- 1–2 slices of lean ham
- 1 portion of cottage cheese
- 1 small portion of low-fat natural yoghurt
- 200 g low-fat quark
- 1 bowl of clear vegetable broth

WEEKS 9–12

In the last three weeks of the plan you can consume slow-release carbohydrates (wholemeal products, pulses) until 6 pm. So during this time you might wish to add these dishes to your lunch or supper menus.

- soya products (only small quantities in the case of any intestinal complaints)
- pulses (for example lentils)
- vegetables and salad
- as an accompaniment: amaranth, buckwheat, millet, corn, quinoa, basmati rice, brown rice, red rice, wild rice or potatoes. You should always bake the potatoes for two hours and then mash them into a puree. That is the preparation method which results in the lowest quantities of starch.
- wholemeal bread
- desserts (see recipes on pages 166–71)
- fresh fruits (as long as the maximum quantities allowed haven't already been consumed, see page 120)

Keep An Eye on your Fruit

Fruit contains an abundance of fructose, and for this
reason it should not be consumed from 2 pm onwards
during the first six weeks of the programme. Until that
time you can consume up to 180 g of berries (blackberries,
strawberries, blueberries, raspberries, currants or
gooseberries) as well as 100 g of fruits that are low
in fructose (for example bananas, apricots, grapefruit,
honeydew melon, sweet limes, mandarins, papaya, peach
or lemon) as well as rhubarb.

DON'T FORGET TO DRINK

It is important that you make sure you drink sufficient liquid: every
day you should consume at least 1.5–2 litres. Preferably, this should
be water, although you can also include herbal or fruit teas.
Insufficient liquid makes the blood more viscous and results in fatigue
and inefficiency.

Establish a Routine

The best approach is to fill up a large flask with herbal tea in the
morning or to get two or three bottles of water ready. That way you'll
be able to see whether you really are drinking enough. A glass of red
wine in the evening is also allowed.

Before you do any sport (and even more importantly afterwards)
don't forget to drink enough. At this point mineral water or a lightly
salted vegetable broth are both ideal, because you need to replace the
minerals that you have lost through perspiration.

The body even needs water during mental exertion. And remember:
thirst is a warning signal to the body, indicating that there is already
a lack of liquid.

HEALTHY THIRST QUENCHERS

Water is, of course, the best substance for quenching your thirst
and rehydrating your body. There are also a number of tasty alternatives.

Flavoured Water

Add a piece of freshly cut ginger, a slice of sweet lime or lemon,
or some fresh herbs like mint or lemon balm to a jug of water.

Herbal Tea

These taste best warm, although some varieties
(like peppermint) are also good cold.

Fruit Tea

Fruit teas make good accompaniments to food. In summer they are
also good when chilled. Fruit teas should be left to draw for around
15 minutes to develop a fuller flavour. Beware: in the evening
the fruit content in the tea can drive insulin levels up.

Maté Tea

This is rich in cell-protecting antioxidants as well as vitamins
A, C, E, B1, B5, riboflavin, biotin, carotene and the minerals magnesium,
calcium, potassium and sodium. It contains less caffeine than black tea
and so is suitable for drinking in the evening.

Rooibos Tea

This tastes blander and rather sweeter than black tea,
contains no caffeine and hardly any bitter substances.

Green Tea

This has a positive impact on cell health (antioxidant) and
cholesterol levels, strengthens the immune system, acts as a protection
against cancer and improves insulin sensitivity.

PLAN YOUR WORK OUT

Exercise is just as crucial to the Sugar Detox Plan as diet. In fact in many ways exercise is a miracle cure in itself; simply incorporating exercise into your regular routine will have a dramatic effect on your overall health and can reduce your risk of major illnesses, such as heart disease, stroke, diabetes and cancer.

You will also find that increasing your activity will help your body adjust to your lower sugar levels more easily, since physical activity can also boost self-esteem, mood, sleep quality and energy.

HOW MUCH IS ENOUGH?

In order to see the best results from the cure, you should try to undertake at least 2.5 hours of exercise a week. And while that might sound exhausting at first it can be divided into manageable daily chunks and spread across a variety of different methods. The best way to achieve your goals is to bring activity into your everyday life, opt to take the stairs when you can, or try walking or cycling instead of driving or taking the bus. Every little thing counts, and the more you do, the better!

For your body to feel the benefit, however, you need to ensure that you raise your heart rate, breathe faster and feel warmer. This will be a different pace for everyone, so one helpful way to tell if you're moving at a decent rate is whether you can still talk, but can't sing!

If you aren't used to exercise then take things easy at the beginning of the cure and follow the suggestions on pages 124–27 from the beginning. If in any doubt you should consult a medical professional before taking on a new exercise regime. Always take care not to overdo it and stop immediately if you feel any pain. Over-exercising can cause your body, metabolism and immune system to suffer, reversing the benefits of exercise. As such, it is important to find the right balance and moderation in your exercise routine, and to allow your body to rest and recover.

Once your fitness levels are improved (or if you are already in good shape) you need to work a little bit harder and incorporate more vigorous activity into your routine through running, aerobics or team sports, for example. If you're working at the right pace you should only be able to say a few words whilst exercising before pausing for a breath.

PREPARATION

It is crucial to warm up properly before beginning your exercise and warm down afterwards. When your body is properly warmed up, your muscles and joints are more flexible, which will save you from stresses and strains, maximize results and make your next bout of exercise even easier. It is important to do some mild aerobic warm-ups before stretching. This raises your body temperature and gets blood flowing more quickly, increasing your muscles' elasticity so they can be stretched without causing damage. Muscles that are tight and constricted work against each other to perform a movement, which means that energy which should be used in the move itself is instead used up by fighting against the muscles themselves, making you feel fatigued more quickly. When stretching, proper breathing control is paramount, as it helps to relax you and increases blood flow throughout your body, improving your range of motion and reducing the risk of injury.

- Stretch calmly and do not jerk – you should only feel a slight tension that subsides after a few seconds.

- Take slow, relaxed breaths, in through your nose and out through your mouth, leaning into the stretch when exhaling, and holding the stretch as you inhale.

- Hold each stretch 20 to 30 seconds, it is even better to time it as accurately as you can.

- Shake your joints gently between exercises for five seconds.

WALKING

Walking is an excellent place to start if you haven't exercised in a while or your fitness levels are currently low. Walking is simple, free and one of the easiest ways to get more active, lose weight and become healthier, no matter your age or energy level. As a low-impact form of exercise, there is less potential for serious injury than with more strenuous activities. Going out for a walk or jog is also a great way to ease the stresses of a day and to enjoy nature and the outdoors.

Week 1: If your fitness levels are low and you are starting the diet plan then don't add exercise for this first week while your body adjusts to a lowered sugar intake.

Week 2: Start with a 15-minute walk or jog each day. You can find a regular time that suits you or alternate times, but the most important thing is that you get out and exercise each and every day.

Week 3: Increase your walk or jog time to 25 minutes, but allow yourself a two minute rest in the middle to get your breath back.

Week 4: Lengthen the time you walk or jog to 35 minutes, retaining a two minute break in the middle if you still feel you need it. If you are still walking try to jog at least some of the distance.

Week 5: Lengthen the time you walk or jog to 45 minutes and try not to take a break in the middle. By now you should be feeling the benefits of your new diet and exercise programme, and you can follow this plan for the remaining 12 weeks, also incorporating additional activities such as swimming and cycling if you feel up to it.

SWIMMING PROGRAMME

Swimming is a brilliant total body work-out, without ever having
to pick up a weight. It's doesn't require any special equipment, other
than a place to do it and the intensity can be gradually increased as
your fitness improves.

Our suggested programme is suitable for those with moderate
to good fitness levels and requires access to a pool or water suitable
for swimming several days a week. If you feel you can do more, or
cannot swim that often during the week, move on to the combined
programme opposite.

Day 1: Warm up by swimming 200 m at a gentle pace. Then increase
your speed and swim as many lengths as you can for 15 minutes
(take a pause of no more than 30 seconds after each 25 m if you feel
you need to).

Day 2: Rest.

Day 3: Warm up by swimming 200 m at a gentle pace. Then swim
breaststroke, backstroke or crawl for 300 m, taking a rest of no more
than 30 seconds after each 100 m. Swim a fast crawl or breaststroke
for 200 m.

Day 4: Rest.

Day 5: Try to swim any stroke for 30 minutes without breaks.

Swimming for Beginners

If your fitness levels are low, then do not swim or incorporate exercise
for the first week that you begin following the Sugar Detox Plan.
In week two follow the programme above but stick to the plan for day
1 and try to repeat it three times a week and move on to following the
whole above programme by week 4.

COMBINED DISCIPLINES

If your fitness levels are good at the start of the programme, then begin with this combined plan (if you already exercise for over 2 hours each week then start at Week 5). You can choose to follow the programme using just one discipline, such as cycling, or mixing and matching activities as suits your schedule best.

Week 1: Start with a jog or light run for 15 minutes each day, or cycle for 20 minutes but try to maintain a speed of 13 km/h (8 mph) or above. Or follow Day 3 of the swimming programme opposite.

Week 2: Increase the length of your exercise to 20 minutes (25 minutes if cycling) and allow a quick break in the middle to catch your breath.

Week 3: Increase the exercise time to 30 minutes (35 minutes if cycling) with just a 2-minute break in the middle. Or follow Day 5 of the swimming programme opposite.

Week 4: Increase your exercise time to 45 minutes (the same for cyclists and swimmers). At this stage it is important to incorporate at least 1 rest day throughout the week to give your muscles time to recuperate and maintain your energy levels.

Week 5: Maintain the programme as for week 5, but try to bring in some challenges. Push yourself to travel further and/or faster, mix up your routine, try a new route and if you are cycling try to ensure you take in some hills.

Week 6: Maintain the programme as for week 5, but, if your schedule allows, increase the length of your exercise to 60 minutes for three days of the week (try to alternate longer and shorter sessions and your rest days).

Week 7–Week 12: Maintain the programme as for week 6 and try to incorporate another form of activity such as an exercise class, swimming session or team sport.

STICKING TO THE PLAN

Our dietary plan cuts down your sugar intake from the very beginning, so the plan essentially stays the same over the entire 12-week period, with only a handful of minor changes every four weeks to ensure that your body doesn't feel starved or become unresponsive.

WEEKS 1 TO 4

In the early weeks it is particularly important to follow the cure rigorously. The more you put into the plan, the better the results will be and the sooner you will see them. Furthermore the harder you try at the beginning the easier the rest will be! Willpower is tough, but stick with it because the results will make you the envy of your friends, as well as giving you a happier, healthier and more efficient body.

It is crucial to listen to your body in these first two weeks to avoid falling victim to your sugar cravings. Your body will learn to reset its metabolic system as quickly as possible, but you might feel a little tired and sluggish at first while your system adapts. If you do feel tired or experience low-energy levels then make an effort to get plenty of rest and drink plenty of fluids. However try not to postpone your daily exercise, the boost of endorphins should start to make you feel better as will the sense of achievement in sticking to the cure.

You should also try to get up at least 45 minutes before breakfast, to allow your body to wake up properly and recognize the feeling of real hunger.

WEEKS 5 TO 8

Your body is slowly getting used to the new dietary regime, and you will no doubt already have noticed that your cravings for sweet things has subsided. This is the first evidence of success on your path away from sugar addiction. Congratulations!

By week 8 you will no doubt have begun to receive some compliments on your new appearance, try to enjoy them and not shrug them off as they will spur you on to completing the cure.

During this period try to get up at least 60 minutes before breakfast. Your diet plan does not call for many changes in these weeks and you should still try hard not to consume any carbohydrates in your evening meals. Keep a close eye on the fruit you are eating and when (see page 120), and remember to drink lots of water.

WEEKS 9 TO 12

Your body has gradually been transformed over the previous weeks and no longer constantly demands sugar. So in the last three weeks of the dietary transition phase, slow-release carbohydrates (wholemeal products, pulses) are allowed up until 6 pm. After that time you should continue to consume just meat, fish and other protein-rich foods as well as vegetables and salad.

WHAT ELSE CAN YOU DO?

Following the sugar-free meal plan will certainly bring a marked improvement to your health and sense of well being. In combination with regular exercise you should be able to see changes to your shape within a few weeks. However there are also some other small steps that can help to magnify the effects of the plan.

Many plants, herbs and roots are rich in protective substances that can help to harmonize a sensitive metabolic processes. These are also more easily absorbed by the body than synthetically produced nutrients and food supplements. By adding these particular ingredients (see the list of natural supplements that are best suited to help with sugar-induced metabolic complaints overleaf) to your regular meals where possible you will be giving your system an extra boost.

NATURAL SUPPLEMENTS AND BENEFICIAL INGREDIENTS

- **Aloe vera** reduces insulin resistance, optimizes sugar absorption, takes care of the insulin receptors and lowers blood sugar. Permitted daily intake: up to 50 g (2 oz).

- **Wild garlic** cleanses the liver and intestine and so eases the strain on the sugar metabolism. Permitted daily intake: up to 50 g (2 oz).

- **Bitter melon** (bitter cucumber) reduces insulin secretion, increases insulin sensitivity and facilitates the absorption of sugar. Permitted daily intake: half a small fruit per day (not during pregnancy).

- **Copalchi bark** protects glycogen stores in the liver, curbs endogenous gluconeogenesis and reduces insulin resistance. Permitted daily intake: up to 5 g (¼ oz).

- **Galangal**, a European variety of ginger, stimulates the metabolic organs, regulates the cardiovascular system and blood pressure levels and enhances our attention and cognitive capabilities. Permitted daily intake: up to 5 g (¼ oz).

- **Guar**, the so-called 'cluster bean', ensures that blood sugar levels rise slowly. In addition only a portion of the sugar is absorbed into our circulation system. Permitted daily intake: up to 20 g (1 oz).

- **Gurmar** is an Ayurvedic plant that reduces sweet cravings, lessens any possible leptin resistance, regulates insulin secretion and so lowers blood sugar levels. Permitted daily intake: up to 20 g (1 oz).

- **Ginger** balances out the cardiovascular system and our blood pressure patterns, it is invigorating, has a positive impact on concentration and alertness and strengthens the immune response system. Permitted daily intake: up to 20 g (1 oz).

- **Cardamom** helps to balance and economize the intestinal and liver metabolisms. In addition some of the substances in this spice help improve the metabolism of carbohydrates and fats. Permitted daily intake: up to 5 g (¼ oz).

- **Coriander** leaves and seeds have detoxifying properties, regulate the immune system, and care for the liver and the intestine. Permitted daily intake: up to 10 g (½ oz).

- **Cumin** acts as an anti-inflammatory, muscle relaxant, liver booster and detoxifying agent. Permitted daily intake: 10 g (½ oz).

- **Rocket's** many bitter substances have a healing effect on the liver. This supports the sugar and fat metabolisms and aids the liver's natural detoxifying activities. Permitted daily intake: up to 100 g (4 oz).

- **Cinnamon** regulates blood sugar, increases the sensitivity of the insulin binding sites, reduces excessive insulin secretion and improves the economic efficiency of the sugar and energy metabolisms. Important: only use true Ceylon cinnamon (cinnamomum zeylanicum). The cheaper cassia cinnamon can damage the liver. Permitted daily intake: up to 2 g (⅛ oz).

Sugar-Free Recipes

38 delicious and nutritious recipes to help you reduce your sugar intake.

JUICES AND SMOOTHIES

Juicing is fast and convenient so it is well worth investing in one of the many efficient models now available on the market. And it can be healthy provided you don't go for the sugar hit that comes with a glassful of orange juice, but think of your juice or smoothie as a balanced meal. In the morning you can mix in your favourite staples likes oats or muesli mixes; at lunchtime go for vegetables, herbs and spices. Here are just a few of our favourites.

SPANISH VEGETABLE SHAKE

Preparation: 15 minutes (plus 1 to 2 hours for chilling)
Serves 2

5 tomatoes, blanched, peeled, deseeded and roughly chopped

1 cucumber, peeled, halved lengthways, deseeded and roughly chopped

1 red and green pepper, washed and roughly chopped

1 small onion, peeled and sliced

1 clove of garlic, peeled and chopped

250 ml tomato juice

Sea salt

Cayenne pepper

Lime juice

2 tablespoons extra-virgin olive oil

2 basil leaves

As you prepare the vegetables, drop them into a blender. After adding the garlic, pour in the tomato juice and blend. Sieve the blended liquid and chill in the fridge for at least one hour. Just before serving, season to taste with salt, cayenne pepper and a squeeze of lime juice. Garnish with a drop of olive oil and a basil leaf.

VEGETABLE BREAKFAST JUICE

Preparation: 5 minutes
Serves 2

250 g beetroot
175 g celery
150 g celeriac
75 g carrots
150 g tomatoes

25 ml wheatgrass or water
1 pinch chilli powder
2 g cinnamon
1 g turmeric

Wash and roughly chop all the vegetables. Blend the beetroot in a
juicer, then add the celery, the celeriac, the carrots and the tomatoes.
If you have a machine that can process wheatgrass, add it now.
Otherwise add a little water to wash through. Season the mix
with chilli powder, cinnamon and turmeric and blend until mixed
thoroughly. Sieve into glasses before serving.

PAPAYA SMOOTHIE

Preparation: 5 minutes
Serves 2

70 g fresh spinach, washed
1 papaya, peeled and deseeded
2 apricots, stoned

1 tablespoon lactose-free milk
50 ml water

Liquidize the spinach with the fruits, the lactose-free milk and the
water. Serve in a tall glass over ice.

KALE AND CARROT SMOOTHIE

Preparation: 3 minutes
Serves 2

1 handful spinach, washed
1 handful kale, washed
2 spring onions, trimmed

Half head of celery, washed
4 carrots, topped and tailed

Start with the greens, because they only make a small amount of juice, which you need to push out with the chunkier roots and stalks. Feed the spinach into the juicer and then the kale. Follow with the spring onions and the celery, one stalk at a time. Finally, add the carrots and mix well before serving in tall glasses.

CARROT AND PEAR SMOOTHIE

Preparation: 2 minutes
Serves 2

4 carrots, topped and tailed
2 conference pears, quartered and cored

Leave the skin on the carrots and pears for added nutrients. Whizz the carrots and pears in a blender and mix well before pouring into glasses. Serve over ice in the summer.

BREAKFASTS

Different definitions of fresh cheeses can be confusing; goat's curd, quark and fromage frais are similar but made through slightly different processes depending on local traditions. The key difference is if they have had a starter culture added that consumes the lactose. Goat and sheep's milk cheeses will also usually have lower levels of lactose.

AVOCADO AND CURD

Preparation: 5 minutes
Serves 1

Pumpkin oil
80 g goat's curd, quark or
    fromage frais
1 ripe avocado, skinned
    and deseeded

1 lemon
Crispbread, to serve
Alfalfa sprouts or
    watercress, to garnish

Add two or three drops of pumpkin oil to the curd and mix well. Slice the avocado flesh and dress with a squeeze of a lemon. Spread the curd on a crispbread and top with the avocado slices. Garnish with alfalfa sprouts or watercress and serve immediately.

BUCKWHEAT MUESLI

Preparation: 5 minutes
Makes 1.5 kg of muesli (45 g per serving)

400 g buckwheat groats
800 g buckwheat flakes
180 g coconut flakes
40 g sugar-free whey
   protein powder

50 g chopped almonds
50 g raisins
Hot water, see method
Lactose-free milk or live
   yoghurt, for serving

Pour the dry ingredients into a large airtight container and stir in
the almonds and raisins. To serve, spoon a portion into a bowl, cover
with hot water and soak for five minutes, before stirring in the milk
or live yoghurt.

FRESH MANGO YOGHURT

Preparation: 10 minutes
Serves 1

Half a mango, peeled and
   roughly chopped
80 g lactose-free
   cottage cheese
40 g quark, curd or yoghurt

120 g berries, rinsed
   and drained
30 g buckwheat groats
1 mint leaf

Place the mango flesh, the cottage cheese and the quark in a tall
container and purée using a hand-held blender. Spoon the quark mix
into a bowl and top with the berries. Sprinkle with buckwheat groats
and garnish with mint.

HERB OMELETTE

Preparation time: 4 minutes
Serves 1

1 tablespoon butter
2 eggs, beaten
Salt and black pepper

1 handful mixed herbs (such
as chives, tarragon, chervil,
or parsley) finely chopped

Melt the butter in a small pan over a medium heat and let it foam.
Pour the egg mixture into the pan and allow to cook for 20 seconds.
Give the pan a swirl so that the egg covers the base and throw in the
herbs. Cook the base of the omelette, while keeping the top a little
runny. Remove the pan from the heat and fold two opposite sides of
the omelette into the centre. Flip over onto a plate and serve with
crusty bread.

*An omelette can really make the most of what is left in the back of the fridge
or the larder to make a fun and nutritious breakfast in a few moments.
Smoked salmon makes it a luxury, spinach gives it iron, and you can
always add other flavours such as mushrooms and cheese (especially hard
mountain cheeses like Comté or Gruyère) or shredded slices of ham or turkey.
Remember that the fresher the eggs the better the omelette.*

SOUPS

If you are cutting down on sugar you need comforting, slow-release metabolizing carbohydrates. Homemade soup is one of the simplest and best ways of bringing them into your diet.

VEGETABLE BROTH

Preparation: 1 hour, 10 minutes
Makes 2 litres

Drink this instead of tea and coffee or use it as a stock for other dishes. Substitute different vegetables depending on the seasons. Leave the skins on any root vegetables that you use.

2 1/4 litres water	2 potatoes, quartered
3 carrots, trimmed and cut into thirds	1 celery stalk, chopped
	50 g diced green onions
2 onions, peeled and quartered	1 head of broccoli
1 leek, washed, trimmed and diced	300 g fresh parsley
	Rock or sea salt

Boil the water in a large pan over a medium heat. Once it is boiling, drop in the vegetables. Trim the top leaves from the parsley and set aside to use as garnish. Add the stalks to the pan. Cover and simmer gently for one hour. Remove the pan from the heat and separate the vegetable broth into two batches. Strain one batch for drinking as a vegetable tea and set the other batch aside to use in your cooking. Serve the leftover vegetables with cold meat or mix with a little mayonnaise for a salad.

SPICY ROOT SOUP

Preparation: 35 minutes
Serves 2

3 tablespoons olive oil

75 g onion, peeled and diced

1/2 teaspoon cumin

1/2 teaspoon paprika

1 pinch cayenne pepper

400 g turnips, washed, peeled
and diced

75 g carrots, washed, peeled
and diced

75 g celery, washed, peeled
and thinly sliced

375 ml vegetable stock

Half a bunch of chives,
washed and sliced into rings

Heat the olive oil in a large saucepan and sauté the onions. Add the cumin, paprika and cayenne pepper. Stir and sauté briefly. Add the turnips, carrots and celery. Pour in the vegetable stock, bring to the boil and simmer over a low heat for 15 minutes. Pour into bowls and sprinkle with chives before serving.

OATMEAL SOUP

Preparation: 20 minutes
Serves 2

80 g oatmeal

400 ml vegetable stock

1 tablespoon butter

1 leek, washed and cut
into rings

Salt and black pepper

4 sprigs of thyme

Nutmeg, for grating

Place the oats in a deep saucepan and fry, without fat, for two minutes over a medium heat. Add the vegetable stock to the oats a little at a time so they absorb the liquid. Melt the butter in a small saucepan, then add the leeks and cook until softened. Add the leeks to the broth and season with salt and a grind of black pepper. Warm through for five minutes more, then season with thyme and nutmeg.

CARROT AND FENNEL SOUP

Preparation: 45 minutes
Serves 4

2 fennel bulbs	2 cloves garlic
1 stick celery	1 litre vegetable stock
1 onion	2 tablespoons crème fraîche
3 tablespoons olive oil	or sour cream
450 g carrots	Salt and black pepper

Thinly slice the fennel, celery and onion and fry in the olive oil until soft but not browned. Peel and chop the carrots and garlic and add to the pan. Cook for another minute or two. Pour in the vegetable stock, bring to the boil, cover and simmer for 20 minutes, until carrots are tender. Remove from the heat and leave to cool slightly before stirring in the crème fraîche or sour cream. Blend the soup until smooth. Taste and adjust the seasoning, then reheat to serve. Top each bowl with a swirl of cream.

BEETROOT CONSOMMÉ

Preparation: 1 hour, 15 minutes
Serves 4

900 g raw beetroot	2 litres vegetable broth
2 carrots	2 teaspoons red wine vinegar
2 turnips	Salt and black pepper

Peel the beetroots, carrots and turnips, and finely chop. Put them into a large saucepan with the stock, bring to the boil and simmer, covered, for 45 minutes, until the vegetables are soft. Strain the soup through a sieve but take care not to press the vegetables – just drain off the clear liquid. If you push the vegetables through, you will end up with muddy consommé! Reheat and season with the vinegar, salt and pepper.

SPINACH SOUP

*This transforms your vegetable broth (see page 142) into a divine soup
suitable for any dinner party. Don't over cook the spinach or you will
lose the vibrant green colour. The broth has already got seven vegetable
flavours, so there is no reason to add anymore, although nutmeg spice is
a classic or, if you are feeling indulgent, add a spoonful of crème fraîche.
If you have a juicer, you can garnish with a few drops of raw spinach juice
to make a surprising contrast. It is quick, simple, nutritious, cheap and
tastes wonderful.*

Preparation: 10 minutes
Makes 1 litre

1 litre vegetable broth
  (see page 142)
2 handfuls spinach, washed

25 ml lactose-free cream
Fennel leaf and spinach
  juice, to garnish

Bring the vegetable broth to a simmer. Add the spinach and allow to
wilt in the heat for one minute. Remove the pan from the heat and
liquidize until smooth. Top off with the cream and pulse one more
time. Season with salt and pepper, and garnish with fennel leaf and
a few drops of raw spinach run through a juicing machine.

BREADS

There is nothing more pleasant than the smell of bread baking in the oven. As you are giving up one old favourite, it can be a good tactic to welcome back another.

CARROT AND CARAWAY LOAF

Preparation: 35 minutes, plus 55 minutes baking time
Makes 1 loaf

660 g spelt flour
330 g buckwheat flour
15 g sea salt
20 g fresh yeast
375 ml lukewarm water

100 g carrots, washed, peeled
and grated
2 tablespoons caraway seeds
Butter, for greasing

Mix the two flours and salt in a bowl. In a second bowl, dissolve the yeast in the lukewarm water. Pour the yeast mixture into the flour and mix well. Transfer the flour and yeast mix to the bowl of a food processor fitted with dough hook and add the grated carrots. Mix well, adding the caraway seeds towards the end. Fashion the dough into a ball with wet hands. Preheat the oven to 170 ˚C. Butter the bottom and sides of a loaf pan. Add the dough ball, cover with a clean kitchen towel and leave to rise for 20 minutes, or until the dough has doubled in size. Slash one centimetre cuts into the risen dough using a sharp knife. Leave for another five minutes, before baking in a hot oven (middle shelf) for 55 minutes.

RYE SOURDOUGH LOAF

Preparation: 3.5 hours (plus souring) and 65 minutes baking time
Makes 1 loaf

930 g rye flour	30 g sea salt
530 ml water	Flour for dusting
42 g fresh yeast	

Mix 210 g of rye flour in a bowl with 230 ml of water. Stir, cover, and sour overnight. The next day, dilute the yeast in 300 ml of lukewarm water. Preheat the oven to 220 °C. In a large bowl mix the yeast, remaining flour and the sea salt. Knead for five minutes and make a round loaf shape, sprinkle with rye flour and leave to rise, covered, on a floured baking sheet for 90 minutes. Bake in the middle of the oven for 20 minutes. Then reduce the temperature to 145 °C. After 45 minutes, turn the oven off and leave bread to settle for an hour.

SPELT BAGUETTE

Preparation: 3 hours (plus proving) and 35 minutes baking time
Makes 1 loaf

660 g spelt flour	20 g fresh yeast
50 g spelt bran	100 g pearl barley flour
330 g wholemeal flour	700 ml cold water

Mix the flours and the spelt bran in a large bowl. Weigh out 950 g of the mix and place in a second bowl (keep the rest for dusting the work surface). Crumble in the yeast and add the cold water. Knead the dough, cover and prove in the refrigerator for 24 hours.

Preheat the oven to 175 °C. Knead the dough again. Lay baking paper on the work surface and sprinkle with the remaining flour. Form a baguette shape and cover with a damp tea towel. Leave to rise for two hours. Transfer the baguette, along with baking paper, to a baking sheet and place in a hot oven. Bake for 35 minutes until crispy.

ANCIENT GRAIN BREAD

Preparation: 45 minutes, plus 60 minutes baking time
Makes 1 loaf

550 g spelt flour
200 g wholemeal flour
100 g barley flour
25 g sea salt

42 g fresh yeast
530 ml warm water
Butter, for greasing

Mix the three flours and the sea salt in a large bowl. In a second bowl, dissolve the yeast in the lukewarm water. Pour the yeast mixture into the flours and mix well. Knead the dough using a food processor with a dough hook, or work it with your hands, until smooth. Preheat the oven to 200 °C. Butter the bottom and sides of a loaf pan. Add the dough, score lightly using a sharp knife and leave to rise for 30 minutes, or until the dough has doubled in size. Place the dough into a hot oven (middle shelf). After 15 minutes, reduce the heat to 160 °C and continue to bake the bread for a further 45 minutes.

One delicious serving idea is 'baker's cucumber sandwiches'. While still warm, cut a slice of ancient grain bread and fry immediately in a non-stick pan without oil. Sprinkle with coarse salt, cover with cucumber slices and garnish with rocket.

SNACKS AND SALADS

These sugar-free snacks and salads are ideal for a quick and easy lunch. They are delicious, healthy and suitable for vegetarians. Most of the recipes use vegetables which are available all year round but you can also experiment with seasonal changes.

BROAD BEAN AND RICOTTA BRUSCHETTA

Preparation: 30 minutes
Serves 4

250 g podded broad beans
3 tablespoons olive oil
Juice 1 lemon
Handful fresh mint
4 slices crusty bread
  (see page 149–51)

Salt and freshly ground
  black pepper
1 garlic clove
140 g ricotta cheese

Bring a pan of salted water to the boil. Plunge the beans into the boiling water, cook for 2 minutes and, using a slotted spoon, scoop the beans out of the hot water and into a bowl of cold water. Peel away and discard the skins. Roughly crush the beans with the olive oil and lemon juice. Chop the mint and mix into the paste. Season with salt and pepper. Toast the bread. Peel the garlic, then rub the crisp surface of the toasted bread with the whole garlic clove. Top each slice of bread with the bean mixture, spoon the ricotta cheese over the bruschetta, and serve.

SPRING VEGETABLES WITH ORANGE AND FENNEL SEEDS

Preparation: 50 minutes
Serves 4

450 g fresh mixed baby
    vegetables, carrots, fennel,
    pak choi, asparagus
1 orange

2 teaspoons fennel seeds
4 tablespoons olive oil
Few sprigs of fresh parsley

Trim and rinse the vegetables – it should not be necessary to peel them, and the carrots are attractive with some of their greenery left intact. Cut any large vegetables into crudité-sized sticks. Juice and zest the orange. Crush the fennel seeds with a pestle and mortar or a rolling pin, mix together with the olive oil, orange juice and orange zest, and combine all the ingredients in a large bowl. Chill for 20 minutes. Chop the fresh parsley and stir into the vegetables before serving.

KALE AND GINGER STIR-FRY

Preparation: 20 minutes
Serves 4

900 g kale, preferably
    cavolo nero
2.5 cm ginger root
½ teaspoon dried red
    chilli flakes

6 tablespoons olive oil
1 tablespoon fennel seeds
Salt and black pepper

Roast the fennel seeds for one minute in a dry frying pan or wok. Then add the oil, grated ginger, chilli flakes and seasoning to the pan and cook for up to three minutes. Add the shredded kale and stir-fry for five minutes. Season to taste with salt and freshly ground black pepper.

BEETROOT SALAD

Preparation: 1 hour, 30 minutes
Serves 2

100 g red beetroot	1 garlic clove
100 g yellow beetroot	1 tablespoon olive oil
50 g beetroot leaves	*Optional*: 1 portion Sour
1 egg	Cream Dressing (below)

Wrap the beetroot in foil and roast slowly for one hour or longer, depending on size. Remove and leave to cool. Bring a pan of water to the boil and cook the leaves and the egg for four and a half minutes – the egg yolk should still be runny. Drain and line up the leaves in a bowl. Peel the egg. Skin the beetroot under running water, rubbing off the skin with your fingers. Then slice thinly into the bowl. Crush the garlic and add the olive oil. Mix in with the leaves and the beetroot. Add the egg – sliced in half, and serve with optional dressing.

SOUR CREAM DRESSING

Preparation: 25 minutes
Makes 750 ml

Half an onion, finely chopped	100 ml wine vinegar
1 garlic clove, finely chopped	3 teaspoons mustard
1/4 leek, washed and sliced	salt, to taste
into rings	350 g sour cream
1/4 bunch of parsley	Salt and black pepper
500 ml canola or hemp oil	

Blend the onion, garlic, leek and parsley with 50 ml of water. Sieve into a pan and bring to the boil. Using a handheld blender, mix the oil with the vinegar, the mustard and the salt. Gradually add the cooled vegetable stock. Stir in the sour cream and season to taste. Pour into a clean bottle and seal well.

MAIN MEALS

When cutting back on sugar it is important to eat a variety of different foods to keep your energy levels raised and to avoid confusing feeling hungry with cravings for sugar.

PEARL BARLEY AND MUSHROOM RISOTTO

Preparation: 40 minutes
Serves 2

5 tablespoons olive oil
80 g red onion, peeled
  and sliced
200 g fine pearl barley,
  rinsed in cold water

750 ml hot vegetable stock
100 g button or chestnut
  mushrooms, cleaned
  and sliced
Fresh herbs to garnish

Preheat the oven to 160 °C. Heat the olive oil in a saucepan and sauté the onions. Add the pearl barley and sauté briefly, stirring all the time. Top up with hot stock and add the mushrooms. Place the risotto, covered, in a hot oven for about 20 minutes. Garnish with fresh herbs, such as fennel, thyme or oregano.

Pearl barley is an especially healthy food and has more benefits than milled white rice. It is especially good for the gut and even thought to lower cholesterol.

LENTIL RAGOUT

Preparation: 45 minutes
Serves 2

300 g puy lentils
1.5 l water
30 g salt, plus more
  for seasoning
20 ml canola oil
15 g rye or spelt flour
75 g carrots, peeled and
  finely diced

75 g celeriac, peeled
  and finely diced
75 g onions, peeled and
  finely diced
500 ml vegetable stock
Salt and black pepper
100 ml sherry vinegar
1 sprig of thyme
1 bay leaf

First cook the lentils. Bring 1.5 litres of water and 30 g of salt to a boil in a large saucepan. Simmer the lentils for 10 minutes then drain and set aside. In a second saucepan, heat the canola oil. Stir in the flour until it begins to tan, then add diced vegetables and sauté. Pour in the vegetable stock and add the hot lentils. Season with salt, pepper and the sherry vinegar. Add the thyme sprigs and bay leaf and cook slowly until just tender, about 10 minutes.

MONKFISH WITH FENNEL TAPENADE

Preparation: 30 minutes
Serves 1

75 g black olives, pitted	2 garlic cloves
75 g green olives, pitted	1 lemon
Half a fennel bulb	Olive oil
2 tablespoons fresh thyme	70 g monkfish fillet

Put the olives and roughly chopped fennel in a food processor. Pick the leaves off the thyme – no stalks – and add those. Peel the garlic and add that. Peel the lemon and add whole. Add a good slug of olive oil and pulse. Check for consistency and add more oil if needed. Leave to infuse. Grill or pan-fry the fish for four minutes each side. Serve with the tapenade, spinach, carrots and steamed potatoes.

BAKED SEA BASS WITH SOY AND GARLIC

Preparation: 40 minutes
Serves 3-4

1 whole sea bass	5 tablespoons soy sauce
2 cloves garlic	5 tablespoons meat or
Small piece of fresh ginger	chicken broth

Wrap your fish whole in silver foil and bake for 30 minutes at 180 °C depending on size. Take out of the oven, check it is cooked through and leave to rest for 10 minutes. Warm a little oil in a small pan and let it heat while you skin and dice the garlic. Drop one small piece into the oil and wait for it to turn brown, then add the rest. Skin the ginger and add to the mix. Watch carefully as it colours, then turn down the heat. Add the soy sauce and the broth. Let it boil once then take off the heat. Portion up your fish and bring the sauce back to the heat so it is hot and dress a little over the fillet. Serve with steamed broccoli and rice

CHICKEN AND GREENS

The great benefit of this recipe is that the juice leftover from the cooking can be used as stock for your soups and other cooking. Everything cooks together in one pot so it is exceptionally easy to make. This dish goes very well with a baked potato.

Preparation: 1 hour
Serves 6

1 chicken, free range	1 head broccoli
1 red onion	150 g Brussels sprouts
2 stalks celery	150 g peas, fresh or frozen
2 leeks	

Lightly oil a casserole. Skin and dice the onion and let fry for a few minutes in the oil. Trim and slice the leeks and celery in to short finger lengths. Make a base in the bottom of the pot and leave to sweat quietly for a few minutes. Snip the string off the chicken so the legs have room. Lay on top of the vegetables. Cover with cold water and bring to a simmer. As it bubbles, turn the heat to low and let it cook slowly for 40 minutes. Prepare the other vegetables. Trim the broccoli and sprouts. Lift out the chicken from the pot and stand on a plate. Add the broccoli and sprouts to the casserole and keep cooking. Give the chicken 10 minutes to cool down while the vegetables cook so that you can handle it easily. Carve off the breasts and the legs and the wings into portion sizes. To serve, add the peas to the casserole and return the chicken pieces to warm through for another 5 to 10 minutes. Serve a piece of chicken with the vegetables and a little juice.

CHICKEN BREAST WITH MILLET COUSCOUS

Preparation: 30 minutes
Serves 2

225 ml chicken or vegetable
  stock
Salt and black pepper
125 g millet couscous
50 g butter
1 tablespoon sherry vinegar

200 g chicken breast, cut
  into strips
2 tablespoons canola oil
Few sprigs of thyme
2 tablespoons sour cream

In a saucepan, season 100 ml vegetable stock with salt and pepper and bring to the boil. Stir in the couscous using a fork, bring to the boil again and then cook over a low heat, stirring occasionally. Melt 30 g of butter in a small saucepan, brown lightly and add to the couscous. Brown the chicken strips in canola oil, remove from the pan and set aside. Melt the rest of the butter in a pan and deglaze with sherry vinegar. Add the remaining vegetable stock and the chicken strips. Season with thyme, salt and pepper and poach the chicken for five minutes. Spoon the couscous onto serving plates, arrange the meat on top and garnish with thyme and sour cream.

ROAST LAMB WITH CREAM OF JERUSALEM ARTICHOKES

Preparation: 3 hours (approx.)
Serves 4

1 shoulder of lamb
   with bone (about 1.2 kg)
3 tablespoons sunflower oil
2 onions, peeled and halved
30 g butter
200 ml vegetable stock
5 Jerusalem artichokes, peeled
   and cut into thumb-sized pieces

100 g cream
25 g cold butter
Salt and black pepper
30 g green peppercorns
3 sprigs rosemary

In a casserole, or in the oven at 200 °C, brown the lamb until it has gone a beautiful colour. Drain off the fat and set aside. Reduce the oven to 120 °C. Once you have peeled and cut the Jerusalem artichokes, place them in cold water to prevent them from discolouring. Place the onion halves in the casserole with the butter. Allow the butter to foam and then add 100 ml of the vegetable stock. Return the lamb to the casserole. Slow-cook for two and a half hours, basting regularly. Simmer the Jerusalem artichokes in a small pan of water for 15 minutes, until soft. Drain and mash with the cream and the cold butter. Season with salt and pepper. Spoon the purée onto a plate and garnish with the green peppercorns and rosemary sprigs. Carve the lamb off the bone and lay on the purée. Dress with a few pan juices.

CONDIMENTS

Traditional sauces, preserves and chutneys are often masking a wealth of hidden sugars. Ketchups in particular can be packed with sugar (sometimes over 20 g per 100 g), so this recipe is a wonderful way to add a flavourful accompaniment to your dishes without piling on the sugar. Similarly this tasty chutney makes a delicious addition to salads and sandwiches without sneaking in the sugar.

TOMATO KETCHUP

Preparation: About 2 hours
Makes 600 ml

4 tablespoons olive oil
200 g onions, peeled and
  finely chopped
2 juniper berries
2 kg tomatoes, blanched,
  skinned, deseeded and
  quartered

1 tablespoon tomato paste
1 clove garlic, minced
1 tablespoon
  sherry vinegar
Salt, to taste

Preheat the oven to 90 °C and sterilize your jars for 20 minutes. Heat the olive oil in a pan and fry the onions. Press juniper berries with a heavy knife and add to the onions. Add the tomato quarters, tomato paste, garlic, sherry vinegar and salt. Simmer, covered, over a low heat for 90 minutes. Pass the ketchup through a sieve and bring to the boil again. Pour into warm sterilized jars.

The sauce keeps in the fridge for up to two weeks. It tastes good with smoked salmon, grilled prawns, carpaccio of veal with raw peppers or salad.

APRICOT CHUTNEY

Preparation: 45 minutes
Makes 600 g (or 3 × 200 g jars)

100 ml coconut oil
500 g red onions, peeled and
   cut into thin strips
50 g yellow pepper, washed
   and cut into thin strips

1.5 kg apricots, washed and
   cut into quarters or eighths,
   depending on size
Salt and black pepper
Sherry vinegar

Preheat the oven to 90 °C and sterilize your jars for 20 minutes. Heat the coconut oil in a pan and sauté the onion and pepper slices over a medium heat. Add two-thirds of the chopped apricots, cover, and simmer for about 20 minutes, until soft. Allow the mix to cool a little, then drain through a colander, reserving the cooking juices. Liquidize the mix roughly so that it keeps some texture, and add the remaining apricots. Warm the mix through a second time. Season with salt and pepper and add the vinegar. If the mix is too dry add a little of the cooking juices back in. Pour into the sterilized jars and seal. Store in the refrigerator or a cool pace.

You can substitute the apricots for peaches, plums or greengages.

DESSERTS

Reducing your sugar consumption does not mean you need to give up on all sweet things. These delicious dessert recipes use some sugar alternatives, such as xylose (sold in the UK as xylitol) and erythritol. They are available to buy online, at supermarkets such as Waitrose, Sainsbury's or Tesco and at health-food retailers such as Holland & Barrett. See page 176 for more information on where to buy. Stockists will be happy to advise you on appropriate brands available in your area and read the product packaging for any additional guidance on use.

CHOCOLATE TART

Preparation: 45 minutes
Makes one 24 cm diameter tart

Shortcrust pastry case
  (see page 168)
300 ml lactose-free milk
300 g lactose-free sour cream
200 g xylitol

240 g dark chocolate
  (minimum 70% cocoa solids)
11 egg yolks

Preheat the oven to 110 °C. Warm the lactose-free milk with the lactose-free sour cream, the xylitol and the chocolate up to 90 °C. Allow to cool down to 80 °C and stir in the egg yolks. Pour the chocolate mixture into the pastry case. Flatten evenly. Bake for 25 minutes in the oven.

VANILLA SPELT PANCAKES

Preparation: 4 minutes, plus 1 minute per pancake
Makes 20 small pancakes

20 g butter
120 g spelt flour
200 ml lactose-free milk
2 eggs
Zest of 1 lemon
Zest of 1 orange

1 vanilla pod, cut in half
   lengthways and seeds
   removed
20 g erythritol (optional)
Oil for frying

Melt the butter in a small pan. In a large bowl, combine the flour, milk, melted butter, eggs, citrus zest, vanilla seeds and erythritol if using. Whisk everything together and leave to stand for ten minutes. Warm some oil in a frying pan over a medium heat and ladle in enough batter mix to cover the base of the pan. Swirl and flip as the pancake sets – in all about one minute. Keep going to use up all the batter, refreshing the oil in the pan if needed.

If desired you can sweeten this mix with 20 g of erythritol or xylitol. Cooked pancakes will keep for around one week in the fridge. Separate them with baking parchment or greaseproof paper. You can also freeze them. Heat them briefly in a microwave.

SHORTCRUST PASTRY

Preparation: 10 minutes, plus 30 minutes for chilling
Makes a 24 cm tart base

200 g plain flour
50 g xylitol

100 g cold butter, cut
into small pieces
2 tablespoons cold water

Pour the flour and xylitol into a large bowl and rub in the butter until it looks and feels like breadcrumbs. Splash the mix with the cold water and form into a ball. Transfer to a flat, floured surface. Roll the pastry out using a rolling pin and short strokes. Give the pastry a quarter turn every so often. Once the pastry is five centimetres larger than your flan dish, lay it in there, pressing it into the corners. Do not cut the edges. Chill for 30 minutes. Preheat the oven to 180 °C. Line the pastry with baking paper and fill with dry beans (pulses) to weigh it down. Bake for 15 minutes. Remove from the oven, lift out the paper and beans and cook for another five minutes. Trim the edges to make it neat.

FRUIT TART

Preparation: 1 hour
Makes one 24 cm diameter tart

Shortcrust pastry case
(see above)
400 g mixed berries, rinsed
150 g xylitol

150 ml lactose-free milk
300 g lactose-free cream
4 eggs

Preheat the oven to 165 °C. Place the berries in a pot over a low heat to warm through briefly. Sprinkle the fruit with 50 g of xylitol and marinate off the heat for 20 minutes. Transfer the fruit to the pastry. Using a whisk, combine the milk, cream, eggs and remaining xylitol in a bowl, stirring until the xylitol dissolves. Pour the mix over the berries and bake the tart in the oven for 45 minutes.

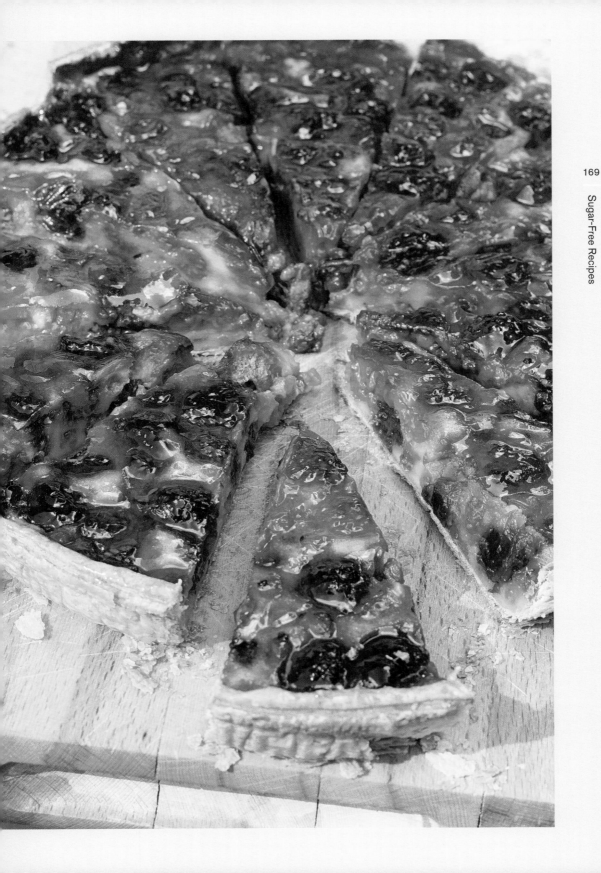

BAKED CHOCOLATE MOUSSE

Preparation: 60 minutes
Serves 6

1 egg
1 egg yolk
10 g erythritol
1 tablespoon xylitol

45 g lactose-free cream
95 g dark chocolate (minimum
70% cocoa solids)

Preheat the oven to 150 °C. Whisk the egg, the extra egg yolk, erythritol and xylitol into a foam. Whisk the lactose-free cream in another bowl, until stiff (an electric mixer makes this quicker, if you have one). Melt the chocolate over a bowl of simmering water and then very slowly stir in the egg mixture. Finally, gently fold in the whipped cream. Line a round, spring-form pan with baking paper. Pour in the chocolate mousse and cover the dish with aluminium foil. Pierce the foil several times using a fork or wooden toothpicks. Bake for 40 minutes. Leave to cool and serve warm. Garnish with mint leaves and raspberries for an extra flourish.

If you use dark chocolate (with a minimum of 70% cocoa solids) and low-fat cocoa powder, nothing will stand in the way of your chocolate fantasy. In fact, dark chocolate actually contains substances that help protect against cardiovascular disease and cancer.

GLOSSARY

Amino acids occur naturally in plant and animal tissues. As the basic constituents of proteins they form the building blocks of life.

Arteriosclerosis is the thickening and hardening of artery walls, a condition that usually occurs in old age.

Beta blockers are medications that inhibit the stimulation of the brain's receptors responsible for cardiac action. They are used to treat angina and reduce high blood pressure, as well as controlling heart rhythm.

Beta-amyloid plaques are clumps of amyloid precursor protein (APP) that accumulate in the brain causing a disruption in and destruction of nerve cells, which are thought by some to lead to Alzheimer's disease.

Body Mass Index (or 'BMI') is an approximate measure of whether you are over- or underweight (see page 53 for how to measure your own BMI).

Blood Sugar Level (sometimes called blood glucose level) is the amount of glucose in your blood. In healthy people this is usually around 4–8 mmol/L (millimoles per litre) although spikes occur following meals. Blood sugar fluctuates more widely for people with diabetes.

Cholesterol is found in most body tissue, the substance and its derivatives contribute to the construction of cell membranes, however concentrations in the blood stream are thought to cause atherosclerosis (fatty deposits in the arteries).

Coeliac disease is a condition in which the small intestine is very sensitive to gluten (a mixture of two proteins found in cereal grains, especially wheat), which can lead to bloating, nausea and difficulty in digesting food. Coeliac sufferers often follow a gluten-free diet to alleviate symptoms.

Disaccharides are sugars in which two monosaccharide molecules are bonded together, such as lactose, maltose, sucrose and isomaltulose (see page 22).

Dopamine is a neurotransmitter (see opposite) that helps to regulate the body's movement and emotional responses.

Enzymes are substances produced by any living organism that act as a catalyst to bring about a biochemical reaction.

Glucagon is a hormone produced by the pancreas that promotes the breakdown of glycogen (the substance deposited in bodily tissues as a store of carbohydrates, see page 31).

Glycaemic index (or 'GI') is a scale of carbohydrate-containing foods based on their effect on blood glucose levels. Foods that are absorbed slowly by the body have a low GI rating, while foods that are more quickly absorbed have a higher rating (see page 24). Consuming more slowly absorbed carbohydrates can help to regulate blood sugar levels.

Hyperglycaemia is a condition in which a sufferer's blood has high glucose levels (see page 33), which may lead to further health complications.

Hypothalamus is an area of the brain that coordinates the control of body temperature, thirst and hunger. It is also involved in sleep and emotional activity.

Insulin is a hormone produced in the pancreas that regulates the amount of glucose in the blood (see page 17). Insulin resistance occurs when insulin levels are sufficiently high over a prolonged period of time causing the body's own sensitivity to the hormone to be reduced (see page 34).

Leptin is a protein produced by fatty tissue, which is believed by some scientists to regulate fat storage in the body (see page 37).

Monosaccharides are single-molecule sugars that cannot be broken to give a simpler sugar. Monosaccharides form the building blocks of longer-chain sugars such as disaccharides and oligosaccharides (see pages 22–3).

Metabolism is the processes that occur within your body in order to sustain life. There are two kinds of metabolism; 'constructive metabolism' which describes the synthesis of proteins, carbohydrates and fats to form tissue and store energy, and 'destructive metabolism' which describes the breakdown of foodstuffs and the body's production of energy and/or waste.

Neurodegenerative describes a condition or state resulting in, or characterized by, degeneration of the nervous system, especially the neurons in the brain

Neurotransmitters are chemical substances that are released by the brain when it receives a nerve impulse. The neurotransmitters transfer the impulse to nerve or muscle fibres, allowing the body to carry out an action or reaction.

Oligosaccharides are carbohydrates whose molecules are composed of a relatively small number of monosaccharide units (see page 22).

Phytochemicals are compounds that occur naturally in plants, some contribute to the colours, flavours or scents of our food. Phytochemicals are not considered essential nutrients, but some are thought to be beneficial to our health (see page 103). Carotenoids, for example, provide colour in plants and our bodies can process them as vitamin A.

Polysaccharides are carbohydrates (such as starch or cellulose) that consist of a number of sugar molecules bonded together (see page 22–3).

Serotonin is a substance found in the body that constricts the blood vessels and acts as a neurotransmitter. It is thought by many to contribute to feelings of happiness and well-being.

Thyroid is a gland in the neck that secretes growth-regulating hormones.

Tryptophan is an amino acid that is an essential nutrient in the human diet and is a constituent of most proteins.

Triglycerides are the main constituents of natural fats and oils, and are also found in your body. When you eat, your body converts any calories it doesn't need to use immediately into triglycerides, which are then stored in your fat cells. Your body then slowly releases these triglycerides for energy as it needs it (see page 98).

INDEX